THEMATIC UNIT
Space

Written by Ruth M. Young, M.S. Ed.

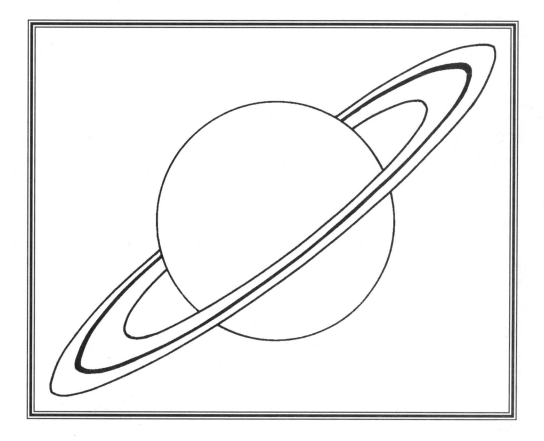

Teacher Created Materials, Inc.
6421 Industry Way
Westminster, CA 92683
www.teachercreated.com

©1996 Teacher Created Materials, Inc.
Reprinted, 2000
Made in U.S.A.

ISBN-1-55734-587-2

Edited by
Mary Kaye Taggart
Walter Kelly

Illustrated by
Howard Chaney

Cover Art by
Marc Kazlauskas

Table of Contents

Introduction

Space contains a captivating, balanced-language, thematic unit. Its 80, exciting pages are filled with a wide variety of lesson ideas and reproducible pages designed for use with intermediate children. This book is divided into three chapters: Astronomy Is Looking Up, We Become Space Travelers, and Touring the Solar System. Each of these chapters has suggestions for supplemental literature which expands the learning of the students on the topics they are studying.

The activities within each chapter are like threads on a loom, weaving together to enable the students to develop their understanding of concepts related to the solar system in which they live. The threads used in this weaving include all areas of the curriculum. Many of these activities are done in cooperative-learning groups to encourage students to exchange and develop their ideas and projects together. Suggestions for interactive bulletin boards and related, extended research projects are provided for the teacher. Furthermore, the culminating activity is a play which applies the students' newly developed understanding of the solar system to create an exciting and informative presentation for other students to enjoy.

This thematic unit contains the following:

- ❏ **literature selections**—summaries of books which relate to the activities in this unit

- ❏ **planning guides**—suggestions for sequencing the activities within each chapter

- ❏ **writing ideas**—suggestions that cross various areas of the curriculum

- ❏ **homework suggestions**—activities to extend into the child's home and involve the family in the excitement of studying about space

- ❏ **curriculum connections**—activities which interweave science, math, language arts, social studies, art, and music to develop the theme of space

- ❏ **group projects**—activities which foster cooperative learning and expansion of ideas

- ❏ **culminating activity**—an activity which applies the knowledge and skills gleaned throughout the unit, thereby assessing students' progress as a result of their study

- ❏ **resource section**—a wealth of information regarding books, sources for materials, reviews of Internet Web sites, and CD-ROMs related to topics in this unit

- ❏ **answer key**—answers for activities used in this unit

To keep this valuable resource intact so it can be used year after year, you may wish to punch holes in the pages and store them in a three-ring binder.

Introduction *(cont.)*

Why a Balanced Approach?

The strength of a whole-language approach is that it involves children in using all modes of communication—reading, writing, listening, illustrating, and doing. Communication skills are interconnected and integrated into lessons that emphasize the whole of language. Balancing this approach is our knowledge that every whole—including individual words—is composed of parts, and directed study of those parts can help a student to master the whole. Experience and research tell us that regular attention to phonics, other word-attack skills, spelling, etc., develops reading mastery, thereby fulfilling the unity of the whole-language experience. The child is thus led to read, write, spell, speak, and listen confidently in response to a literature experience introduced by the teacher. In these ways, language skills grow rapidly, stimulated by direct practice, involvement, and interest in the topic at hand.

Why Thematic Planning?

One very useful tool for implementing a balanced-language program is thematic planning. By choosing a theme with correlating literature selections for a unit of study, a teacher can plan activities throughout the day that lead to a cohesive, in-depth study of the topic. Students will be practicing and applying their skills in meaningful contexts. Consequently, they tend to learn and retain more. Both teachers and students will be freed from a day that is broken into unrelated segments of isolated drill and practice.

Why Cooperative Learning?

Besides academic skills and content, students need to learn social skills. This area of development cannot be taken for granted. Students must learn to work cooperatively in groups in order to function well in modern society. Group activities should be a regular part of school life, and teachers should consciously include social objectives as well as academic objectives in their planning. For example, a group working together to solve a problem may need to select a leader. Teachers should make clear to the students the qualities of good leader-follower group interaction just as they would state and monitor the academic goals of the project.

Four Basic Components of Cooperative Learning

1. *In cooperative learning, all group members need to work together to accomplish the task.*

2. *Cooperative learning groups should be heterogeneous.*

3. *Cooperative learning activities need to be designed so that each student contributes to the group and individual group members can be assessed on their performance.*

4. *Cooperative learning teams need to know the social as well as the academic objectives of a lesson.*

Astronomy Is Looking Up

Summary

This first chapter will lay the foundation for those which follow. It will provide a summary of astronomy through the eyes of the early astronomers, dating back 2,000 years to explain the origins of the science. Activities in this chapter will enable students to experience some of what these early astronomers discovered before and after the invention of the telescope. These observations of the day and night sky shaped their theories. Some of the major theories of the earliest astronomers were inaccurate but set the thinking of most people for 1,500 years. Great courage was required by the astronomers of the 15th and 16th centuries to challenge these theories, then endorsed by some of the dominant religions of that period. Through a variety of activities, students will see how these theories evolved and changed into what we believe about our solar system today.

Overview of Activities

The lessons in this chapter include simple experiments and activities which supplement the study of early astronomers, interweaving the history of astronomy with the science. Students will better appreciate these astronomers as they learn about their lives and work, followed by activities which highlight their theories, observations, and discoveries.

Setting the Stage

Students may work in cooperative groups to gather information about some of the early astronomers. They should use a minimum of three different sources for their information, including Web sites if computer Internet access is available. Provide ample resources and time for students to prepare a quality presentation for the class.

Let students make their presentations about their astronomers, taking them in chronological order. Intersperse the appropriate activities between these reports. These are as follows:

Ancient Astronomers

- *Following the Sun:* The earliest astronomers learned about the motion of the sun by using a shadow. From this came the simple sundial, as well as data that showed the height of the sun at noon and rising and setting positions as they changed during the year.

- *Pictures in the Sky:* The earliest astronomers discovered that the planets, sun, and moon appeared to stay within the narrow band of stars which run east-west across the sky. They divided this path into 12 sections and created patterns with the stars along the path to form the zodiac constellations. This formed a star map which helped them to identify and predict the locations of the planets, moon, and sun which moved within this path.

Early Astronomers

- *Planets on the Move:* Before the telescope was invented, Tycho Brahe and other astronomers gathered information about the location of the planets within the zodiac constellations. This detailed data helped astronomers like Johannes Kepler and Sir Isaac Newton develop models for the solar system to explain these motions.

- *By the Moons of Jupiter:* Galileo used a telescope and discovered that the moons of Jupiter orbit that planet, not Earth. This disproved the generally accepted theory of his day that the Earth was in the center of the known universe.

Astronomy Is Looking Up *(cont.)*

Supplemental Books

The two books described below would be excellent supplements to the lessons in this chapter. (Publication information is located in the Resources section, page 77.)

Exploring the Night Sky by Terence Dickinson

This beautiful book is divided into three sections: A Cosmic Voyage, Alien Vistas, and Stargazing. It can serve as a great supplement for this chapter (Astronomy Is Looking Up) and Touring the Solar System at the end of this thematic unit. There are fantastic photographs and art throughout this award-winning book.

Use the section Stargazing (pages 48–69) which describes how to recognize planets, stars, and constellations. Included is information on how to locate various seasonal constellations by using the Big Dipper and Little Dipper. Charts and pictures in this chapter will enhance student understanding of how to enjoy looking at the night sky. The last section of this chapter gives information on using telescopes and binoculars to study the sky.

The Night Sky by Dennis Mammana

This book is written to guide young observers of the sky. There are many great activities which will expand some of those found in this chapter. It gives helpful hints for observing the sky, including sky maps for the four seasons. Simple explanations of the zodiac and stories about some of the constellations are provided. Sections of this book will also be useful in the other chapters in this thematic unit.

Use chapters 1–5 from *The Night Sky,* which describe the sun, stars, and planets, as well as the rotation and revolution of Earth. This includes hints on observing the night sky, as well as seasonal star charts to reproduce for students.

Extending This Chapter

- If a planetarium and/or observatory are available, make arrangements to take the students so they can apply what they are studying in class.

- Schedule observing sessions for the evenings for students and their families. Have them bring binoculars or telescopes if they have them. Select a dark site away from city lights if possible. Check the newspaper, almanac, Web sites, or sky calendars (see Resources section) to find when there will be planets in the evening sky. Try to pick a night when there will be a moon that is between four and 10 days past the new phase; this will avoid the brighter moon that will blot out dim stars and planets. Bring star charts and a bright flashlight to point out the constellations. Winter is the best time to observe because during this season there are many outstanding large constellations, such as Orion, and the sky gets dark earlier.

- Visit the Web sites listed in the Resources section to let students glean more information from the Internet about the topics covered in this chapter.

- Invite a professional or amateur astronomer to talk to the class about his or her career or hobby. Many astronomers decided upon their career simply because early in life they became fascinated observing the day and night skies. It can also become a lifelong hobby, even without expensive equipment like a telescope.

Ancient Astronomers

Teacher Information: Each day when we observe the sky, it appears that the sun moves around Earth, rising in the east and setting in the west. The stars and moon follow this same daily motion. So it is easy to see why the first astronomers thought Earth was in the center of everything. Even the "wandering stars," which they named planets, rode the sky in this same path. The Greek philosoper Plato (428–347 B.C.) believed no observations were needed to understand nature, only reasoning. He reasoned that the sun, moon, and planets were on spheres moving in combinations of circular motions around Earth. His student Aristotle (c. 384–322 B.C.) taught this theory to his student, Alexander the Great. Ptolemy (A.D. c. 100–165), another ancient Greek astronomer, constructed a model of the planets' motions around Earth based on the ideas of Plato and Aristotle. His model was so accurate it could predict planetary positions and was believed by most people for 1,500 years.

Materials: information cards (page 8), Ancient Astronomers Report (page 9), reference books, Web site information on astronomy, any other items needed to present reports

Lesson Preparation:

1. Gather resources for students to research the lives of ancient astronomers. Some astronomers will have less information available about them; thus, many reference sources will be needed.

2. If access to the Internet is available, bookmark the following Web sites which students can visit. The first Web site is an index of ancient Greek astronomers. The next Web site includes links to information about Ptolemy and Aristotle.

   http://www.csd.uch.gr/~vsiris/ancient_greeks.html
   http://es.rice.edu/ES/humsoc/Galileo/People/tycho_brahe.html

Procedure:

1. Divide students into six cooperative groups and distribute the Ancient Astronomers cards.

2. Discuss what is expected of them during this research project:

   • Use a minimum of three sources of information.
   • Develop a presentation telling about these astronomers and include information about the history of their time.

3. Use the following suggestions and those of your own to encourage students to do more than just the standard report.

   • Present a video with students impersonating ancient astronomers. Describe their theories, using drawings and models.
   • Create a choral reading to bring their astronomers to life, including pictures or models to illustrate what they did or their theories.

4. Introduce references you have to help in their research.

5. Send notes to parents informing them of their children's projects and asking them to help find additional resources at the local library or on the Internet.

6. Permit sufficient time for students to collect information and develop creative presentations.

7. Do the Following the Sun (page 10) and Pictures in the Sky (page 12) activities. These will be more effective after the presentations.

Closure:

Conduct student presentations with an audience of parents or other students. This will encourge students to do their best.

Ancient Astronomers *(cont.)*

Aristotle (Greek, 384–322 B.C.)

Interesting Facts:

Student of Plato and later became a teacher to Alexander the Great. Did not do any experiments or observations since he believed one could reason explanations for what happened in nature. Decided that Earth must be a sphere since it cast a curved shadow on the moon during a lunar eclipse. Many thought it was flat at this time.

Hipparchus (Greek, c. 180–125 B.C.)

Interesting Facts:

Measured star positions and put together a catalog of about 850 stars, including showing their brightness. He used observations of star locations made 160 years before and discovered that they had changed location in the sky. He decided that this was caused by Earth wobbling as it spun on its axis like a top, so the stars would appear to gradually shift. He was correct.

Ptolemy (also *Claudius Ptolemaeus*)
(Greek, A.D. c. 100–125)

Interesting Facts:

Developed detailed models of the known universe, based on the theories of Plato and Aristotle. This showed Earth in the center with the sun, moon, planets, and stars fixed to spheres which orbited our planet. Even though his Earth-centered model was wrong, it was so accurate that it could predict the location of planets and was believed for 1,500 years.

Aristarchus (Greek, 310–230 B.C.)

Interesting Facts:

Observed that the sun was much larger than the moon or Earth. Decided that the sun, being the larger, was most likely the center of the universe, not Earth. Since he could not show any evidence to prove his idea, most ignored him and went on believing that Earth was the center of the universe.

Eratosthenes (Greek, c. 276–195 B.C.)

Interesting Facts:

Measured the angle of the shadow from a pole at noon on the first day of summer. He knew that at the same time there was no shadow at another city 500 miles away. Using geometry, he divided 360 degrees by the 7 degrees angle and then multiplied that percentage of the circle times 500 miles. He calculated the circumference of the Earth at 28,000 miles. It is actually 24,860 miles, so he was very close.

Plato (Greek, 428–347 B.C.)

Interesting Facts:

Perhaps the most famous teacher and philosopher of all times. He profoundly influenced the thinking of his students, including Aristotle. Plato stated that the world was composed of only four elements: air, water, fire, and earth. He was not correct, but his students believed him.

Ancient Astronomers Report

Student Team: _____

Instructions: Copy the information from the Ancient Astronomers card you received. Use at least three resources to add new information about this person. Make notes about what he did or theories he developed. Include reference sources and note where to find pictures or drawings you may want to use in your final report.

Name of Ancient Astronomer: _____

Nationality: _____ **Lived:** _____

Interesting Facts:

_____

_____

_____

New Facts	**Reference Sources***
_____	_____
_____	_____
_____	_____
_____	_____
_____	_____
_____	_____
_____	_____

*Include the title, author, publisher, date of publication, and pages you used for each reference. If you used Web sites, be sure to list the exact addresses and any pictures or drawings you may want to use in your report.

Final Suggestions: On another paper, plan the details of how you will present your report. Think of how to make it both interesting and filled with correct information that will bring your ancient astronomer to life.

Following the Sun

Teacher Information: Students make a record of the sun's motion during one day, using the shadow of a stick just as early observers did. This will tell them much about the sun's motion across the sky, including changes in altitude and speed of motion. Once the record is made, it should be repeated once a month to compare the records and see the changes of the sun's path throughout the year.

Materials: 4' x 3' (122 cm x 91 cm) white butcher paper, perpendicular stick (e.g., ring stand), black marker, black yarn

Lesson Preparation:

1. On a sunny day before school, tape butcher paper to a paved area that will remain in the sunlight all day. Align the paper lengthwise to point east-west. Tape the paper so it will not blow away. Place the stick perpendicular to the ground on the south edge, midway across the paper. Write the date and directions on the paper.

2. Use the marker to mark the tip of the shadow on the paper with a dot and then record the time next to the dot.

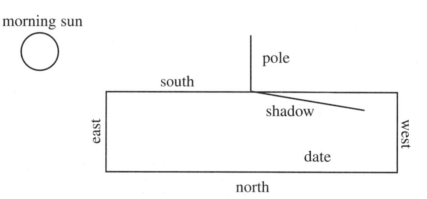

Procedure:

1. Tell students they are going to make a record of the sun's motion, using a shadow of a stick as astronomers did thousands of years ago. Where the paper has been spread out, point out the shadow on the paper. Mark the tip of the shadow and write the time next to this new dot. Show where the earlier mark was made and have students discuss what they notice (e.g., *the present shadow has moved toward the east*). Ask them to explain this. (*Most will say the sun has moved west; accept that answer for now.*) They will notice that the shadow has moved since it was last marked. Mark the new location of the shadow and point out how swiftly it moves.

2. Assign different students to return to this location each hour to mark the shadow with a dot and the time.

3. Before school ends, return to the shadow record to discuss it. Use black yarn to recreate the shadow by tying a strand to the shadow pole and stretching it to the dot. Cut it off and tape it over the dot. Do this for each shadow location. Have students study this record and tell you what they see has happened. (*The shadow has continued to move eastward, but its length has changed. It was long in the morning, becoming shorter until mid-day when it began to get longer again in the afternoon.*)

4. Ask them to explain these changes. Many will conclude that the sun has moved across the sky, getting higher until mid-day, then lower in the afternoon. Tell them when people saw this long ago, they believed it was the sun moving around Earth. The stars and planets seemed to do the same during the night. Until the 1600s, most people believed Earth was in the center of everything they could see in space. (Refer to their ancient astronomer reports.)

Following the Sun *(cont.)*

Closure:

Explain that it is impossible to feel Earth move, even though it is actually rotating at about 1,000 miles per hour at the equator and slower as you move north or south from the equator. This spinning of Earth west-to-east makes the sky appear to be moving around us east-to-west. Have the students stand in one spot and then pretend they are Earth rotating slowly in a counterclockwise motion. Tell them to watch objects around them as they do this and they will see them move in the opposite direction.

Explain that other activities in this unit will show them how later astronomers dared to suggest that the sun was in the center of the solar system. Eventually, they could look at other planets with telescopes to prove that Earth was not in the center.

Extender:

Make a record of the sun's motion on approximately the same date each month. Use a piece of white 8 ½" x 11" (22 cm x 28 cm) paper mounted on cardboard rather than the larger butcher paper. Place a T pin through one edge of the cardboard and tape it in a perpendicular position. Place the paper over the pin and tape it at the corners. Label the paper with the date and directions. Put this record in sunlight on a table and mark the shadow of the pin with a dot at about hourly intervals throughout the day. Complete each record by drawing lines from the pin's hole in the paper to the dots.

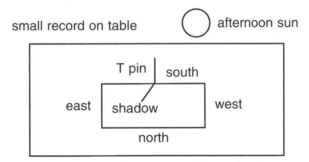

As it is completed, post each record in the classroom for the students to see. As they compare these, they will see that the pattern of shadows will change in a similar way to those shown below.

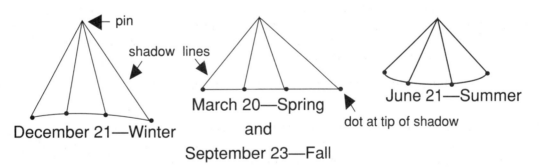

The shadows in winter are longest since the sun rides at its lowest in the sky. Just the opposite happens in summer: the sun rides at its highest in the sky, and thus shadows are shortest. During spring and fall, the sun's path across the sky is at the midpoint. The shadows are between the longest and shortest recorded in winter and summer. The curvature which appears when the shadow dots are connected is due to the path of the sun being high, low, or in between. The shadows will vary in length, depending upon where you are on Earth. Near the equator, the sun rides higher in the sky than it does in latitudes farther north or south throughout the year. The shadows at the equator will not become as long or short as they do in latitudes farther north or south.

Pictures in the Sky

Teacher Information: Constellations are images of human and animal figures in the sky, using the stars much like a dot-to-dot picture. They were originally distributed symmetrically around a point directly above Earth's North Pole at that time. Since Earth wobbles like a top, the axis gradually shifts in a circular motion over 26,000 years. This is called *precession*. Astronomers have used their knowledge about precession to calculate that the constellations were most likely invented nearly 3,000 years ago.

Many of the constellations were figures of mythology fitted into star patterns and, therefore, do not always look like the figures they represent. For example, the stars forming Sagittarius the Archer look more like a teapot than an archer with bow and arrow.

The 12 zodiac constellations are located along the path Earth follows around the sun, called the *ecliptic*. The sun, moon, and planets are seen against the background of these constellations. Astronomy had its beginnings in astrology in which human behavior was supposedly controlled by the motion of the planets, sun, and moon within the zodiac constellations. Early astrologers carefully recorded the changing locations of these celestial bodies, valuable data that later helped astronomers understand much about these motions. Scientists realize there is no connection between how these celestial bodies move and what happens to anyone on Earth. Zodiac and other constellations serve as a useful sky map, helping us locate planets, comets, and other celestial bodies. For example, monthly charts show locations of planets within constellations. Learning these constellations can help students locate them and the planets which move among the star patterns.

The dates when the sun is in each zodiac constellation (pages 14 and 15) do not match dates you will see in horoscopes since these charts were made long ago when the sun was in different constellations. The sun's position changes against these constellations since Earth does not return to exactly the same place in its orbit at the same time each year. The months stated on the pictures are astronomically correct for the location of the sun at this time.

Materials: zodiac constellations (pages 14 and 15), overhead projector, 12 sheets of large black construction paper, chalk or white grease pencil, clamp-on light fixture with 150-watt bulb

Lesson Preparation:

1. Make transparencies of the zodiac constellations. Project them individually onto the large black paper and use the white marker to trace the stars (dots) and lines. The sizes of the dots denote brightness, not star size. Larger dots represent brighter stars.

2. Include the name of the constellation as well as when the sun is there and when it can be seen.

3. Find a large room for this lesson. Use a string 4-feet (122 cm) long with a loop at one end and a piece of chalk tied to the other to make a circle in the center of the floor. Have someone hold the loop on the string in the center of the floor, stretch out the strings, and use the chalk to draw a circle. Shorten the string to 2.5 feet (76 cm) and draw another circle within the first, using the same center point. Place the clamp-on lamp in the center of these circles above the level of your head, if possible.

Pictures in the Sky *(cont.)*

Procedure:

1. Describe the information about the zodiac constellations, using the transparencies to enable students to see what they look like.

2. Select 12 students to hold the zodiac constellation pictures. Space them equally around the large circle. The constellations should be in numerical order, clockwise around the circle.

3. Place remaining students around the inner circle, facing the constellations. Turn on the bright light and turn off the room lights. Tell them that the bright light is the sun and they are the Earth. Have them spin slowly in their positions in a counterclockwise direction. Day is when they face the sun; night is when they face away from the light and see the stars.

4. Explain that if they could go out beyond the solar system, they would see that Earth moves counterclockwise around the sun. Let them walk slowly in a counterclockwise direction around the circle, looking at the stars. Point out that the constellations appear to change as they move. From Earth they see new constellations gradually appearing in the eastern sky as those in the west gradually disappear below the western horizon. It takes 12 months to get back to the original set of constellations. Have them walk around the circle until they return to the constellation they saw at first. Explain that they have just gone through one year.

5. Tell them to turn toward the sunlight and try to see the constellations beyond. Explain that the sun is so bright we can't see the stars beyond it. Tell the students that the 12 zodiac constellations correspond to the location of the sun during each of the 12 months. When the sun is "in" one of them (e.g., Leo), we can't see that constellation. Only when we go into space where sunlight is not scattered by Earth's atmosphere, can we see the stars and sun together. Even then, some of the stars near the sun are hard to see. We can also catch glimpses of bright stars and planets during a total solar eclipse when the sun is blotted out by the moon and we can see outer space beyond our atmosphere.

6. Explain that the planets and moons move around the sun on a plane, like a huge dinner plate with the sun in the center. The zodiac constellations lie beyond this plane and appear roughly east-west across Earth's sky. The planets, moon, and sun never appear in the sky north or south of this band of stars.

7. Describe the history of constellations and the connection between astrology and astronomy. Be sure to tell them that scientists today know that the movements of the planets, sun, and moon within the zodiac constellations do not control our lives.

Closure:

Distribute the zodiac constellations and have students look at the figures the star patterns are supposed to represent. Ask them which ones most resemble the pictures. These are Leo (the lion), Scorpius (the scorpion), and Taurus (the bull—face and horns only).

Extender:

Enlarge copies of some constellations without the lines and have the students make their own constellations. Have them use the patterns of the stars (dots) to turn them into pictures of things familiar to them.

Zodiac Constellations

To the Student: The 12 constellations in these pictures are those which appear along the path the sun seems to follow in the sky as Earth moves around it. Long ago people thought that our lives were controlled by the location of planets in these constellations. Today, we know that the planets move in orbit around the sun and have no influence on humans at all. The shapes of constellations form a useful map of the sky which helps us locate planets which are seen against these stars. A planet looks like an extra star in a constellation, but it gradually moves into the next constellation.

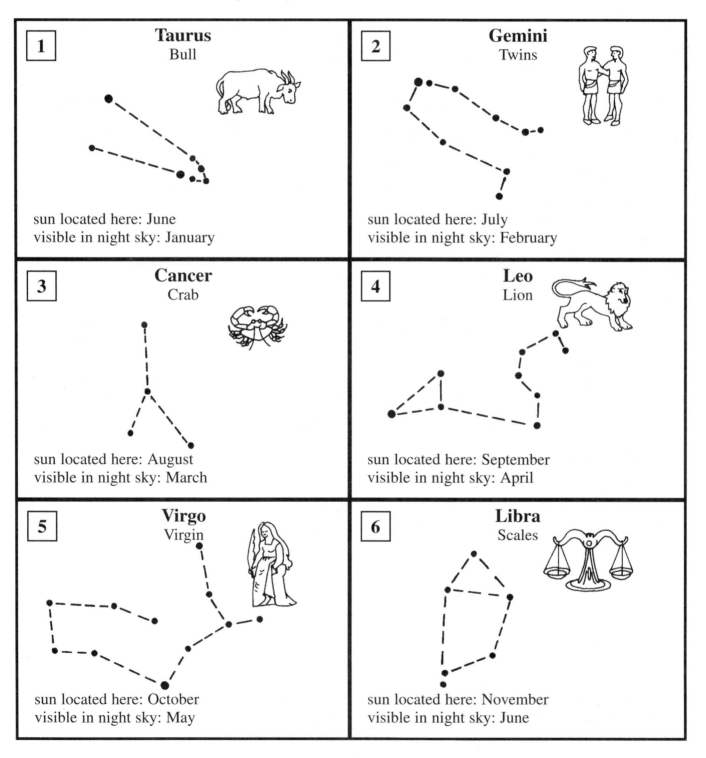

1 **Taurus**
Bull

sun located here: June
visible in night sky: January

2 **Gemini**
Twins

sun located here: July
visible in night sky: February

3 **Cancer**
Crab

sun located here: August
visible in night sky: March

4 **Leo**
Lion

sun located here: September
visible in night sky: April

5 **Virgo**
Virgin

sun located here: October
visible in night sky: May

6 **Libra**
Scales

sun located here: November
visible in night sky: June

14

Zodiac Constellations *(cont.)*

The time on a card stating when a constellation is visible is the best month to see it. However, it will also be visible the month before and after. Visibility of these constellations also depends on the latitude of your location.

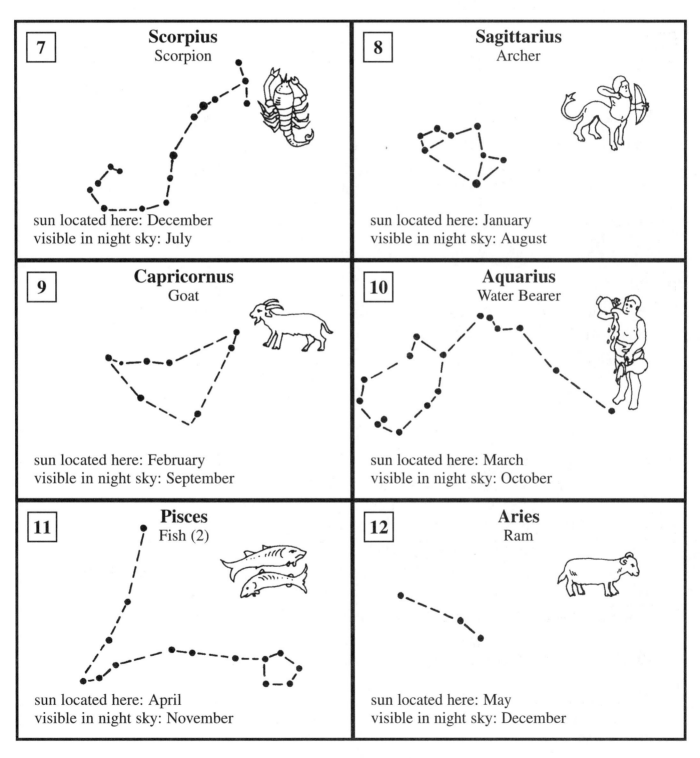

7 **Scorpius**
Scorpion

sun located here: December
visible in night sky: July

8 **Sagittarius**
Archer

sun located here: January
visible in night sky: August

9 **Capricornus**
Goat

sun located here: February
visible in night sky: September

10 **Aquarius**
Water Bearer

sun located here: March
visible in night sky: October

11 **Pisces**
Fish (2)

sun located here: April
visible in night sky: November

12 **Aries**
Ram

sun located here: May
visible in night sky: December

Early Astronomers

Teacher Information: In the 15th century during the Renaissance, new ideas began to surface in Europe. Important scientific studies began at major universities, increased exploration by sea required better celestial navigation, and ideas were now spreading via the newly-invented printing press. These ideas often challenged long accepted "truths" about Earth, dating from Ptolemy's model of the known universe 1,500 years before this. Only the most courageous scientists were willing to risk possible imprisonment, torture, and death for writing about the discovery that it was the sun occupying the center of the planets, not Earth. Their writings helped others build on their observations and calculations to prove that the sun was the center of our solar system.

Materials: information cards (page 17), Early Astronomers Report sheet (page 18), reference books and Web site information on astronomy, other items needed to present reports

Lesson Preparation:

1. Gather resources for the students to use as they research the lives of early astronomers.

2. If access to the Internet is available, bookmark the following Web site which students can visit to gather information about Brahe, Copernicus, Galileo, Kepler, and Newton. This includes drawings and pictures about the scientists and their work, as well as maps and other data about the periods in which they lived.

   http://es.rice.edu/ES/humsoc/Galileo/People/tycho_brahe.html

Procedure:

1. Divide students into six cooperative groups, and distribute the Early Astronomers cards to them.

2. Discuss what is expected during this research project.

   - Use a minimum of three sources of information.
   - Develop interesting presentations telling about these astronomers.
   - Include information of the times during which these astronomers' lived.

3. Use the following suggestions and those of your own to encourage students to do more than just the standard report.

   - Present a TV talk show with the early astronomers being impersonated by one member of each group. Tell about their theories, using drawings and models.
   - Create a skit which will bring the astronomers to life, including pictures or models which may help illustrate what they did or their theories.

4. Introduce the reference sources you have collected to help them in their research.

5. Send home a note to parents informing them of their child's responsibility and requesting that they help find additional resources at the local library or on the Internet.

6. Permit sufficient time for students to collect information and develop creative presentations.

7. After the presentations, do the activities related to early astronomers—Planets on the Move (pages 19–22) and By the Moons of Jupiter (pages 28 and 29).

Closure:

Conduct student presentations, providing an audience of parents or other students. This will encourage students to do their best.

Early Astronomers *(cont.)*

Tycho Brahe (Danish, 1546–1601)

Interesting Facts:

He made observations on a regular basis, using his eyesight, astrolabes, and quadrants to make the most accurate measurements yet of planets. His observations proved that the old tables used to predict the positions of the planets were wrong. He observed a supernova (exploding star), which disproved the accepted belief that nothing changed in the heavens beyond the orbit of the moon. He still believed Earth was in the center of the known universe.

Galileo Galilei (Italian, 1564–1642)

Interesting Facts:

He did not invent the telescope but did use one he built to look at the moon, sun, and planets out to Saturn. He discovered that the moon was not smooth but had mountains and craters, the sun had sunspots, and the planet Jupiter had four moons which revolved around it. Most believed that all these were smooth spheres and revolved around the sun. The Catholic Church believed his theories were against the Bible and excommunicated him.

Johannes Kepler (German, 1571–1630)

Interesting Facts:

He was assistant to Tycho Brahe and, using his data about Mars, discovered that the orbit had to be an ellipse, not a circle. This was against the belief that everything in space moved around Earth in perfect circles. He was the first astronomer to believe in Copernicus' theory. He discovered the three laws of planetary motion which explained how planets move in orbits around the sun.

Nicholas Copernicus (Polish, 1473–1543)

Interesting Facts:

Developed the theory that Earth moves around the sun along with all the other planets. During his lifetime most people believed Earth was the center of the universe. He could not prove his theory, but his explanation for the motion of the planets around the sun was less complicated and mathematically stronger than that of Ptolemy. He is considered the founder of modern astronomy.

Edmund Halley (English, 1656–1742)

Interesting Facts:

First to calculate the orbit of a comet he observed in 1682, he proved that the comet was the same one which had been seen by astronomers in 1531 and 1607. He predicted it would return in 1758. It appeared on Christmas Day that year and was named Halley's Comet. It returns about every 77 years. He also mapped the stars of the southern hemisphere, studied the moon's effects on tides, and measured the distance from Earth to the sun.

Sir Isaac Newton (English, 1642–1727)

Interesting Facts:

He used the work done by Kepler to develop his theories of universal gravity, stating that each one of every pair of bodies pulls on the other. He also said that the strength of the pull (gravity) depended upon the amount of matter in the objects and the distance between them. This explained how planets and their moons could remain in space while revolving around the sun. Edmund Halley convinced Newton to publish his findings.

Early Astronomers Report

Student Team: _____

Instructions: Copy the information from the Early Astronomers card you received. Use at least three resources to add new information about this person. Make notes about what he did or new ideas he developed. Include reference sources and note where to find pictures or drawings you may want to use in your final report.

Name of Early Astronomer: _____

Nationality: _____   **Lived:** _____

Interesting Facts:

_____

_____

_____

New Facts	**Reference Sources***
_____	_____
_____	_____
_____	_____
_____	_____
_____	_____
_____	_____
_____	_____
_____	_____

*Include the title, author, publisher, date of publication, and pages you used for each reference. If you used Web sites, be sure to list the exact address and any pictures or drawings you may want to use in your report.

Final Suggestions: On another paper, plan the details of how you will present your report. Think of how to make it both interesting and filled with correct information that will bring your early astronomer to life.

Planets on the Move

Teacher Information: Ancient astronomers observed and named five planets: Mercury, Venus, Mars, Jupiter, and Saturn. These planets appeared to move east-to-west each night, like the stars and moon. However, each day the planets, sun, and moon appeared to move slowly eastward against the background of stars. Some planets moved faster than others. Sometimes these planets appeared to slow down, stop, and then change directions, moving westward or backward through the stars. This was called *retrograde* motion. Ptolemy's model explained retrograde motion by having the planets orbit Earth in a series of smaller circles (epicycles) with the center of these circles following a larger circle around Earth. In 1554 Nicholas Copernicus put forth a bold plan, breaking with the Ptolemaic system. Copernicus suggested that the sun, not Earth, was in the center of the planets. Since he could not prove this, most people continued to believe the theory developed by ancient astronomers over 1,500 years earlier.

About 1575, Tycho Brahe used special instruments to make careful measurements of where planets were night after night. Tycho Brahe found Ptolemy's model did not always predict the planets' locations exactly. However, he could not prove that Earth moved, so he doubted that Copernicus' model was correct. He combined the two models to fit his observations by having the moon orbit Earth and all the planets orbit the sun, which in turn orbited Earth.

Materials: transparencies of the Constellation Chart (pages 23 and 24), 1997 Planet Data (page 22), Early Theories of the Planetary System (page 25), Mars in Retrograde (page 26), Mars in Retrograde Answers (page 27); white butcher paper 3' x 5' (91 cm x 152 cm), black permanent marker, rulers

Lesson Preparation:

1. Tape the edges of the Constellation Chart transparencies together so the ecliptic matches at the 0 degrees mark. Project the complete Constellation Chart onto the butcher paper so it fills the paper. Trace every part of the chart onto the paper, using pencil; then go over the pencil with permanent marker and put the chart on a bulletin board.

2. Make eight copies of the 1997 Planet Data and number the copies. Highlight data to be plotted on the chart by groups 1–8. Assign to a different group half the data for each planet being charted.

3. Make a copy of the Constellation Chart and tape it together like the transparency. Use this copy to plot the data for all four planets and to use as a reference to check the students' work.

1997 Planet Data for First of Each Month							
Month	**Venus** Constellation		**Mars** Constellation		**Jupiter** Constellation		**Saturn** Constellation
January	Ophiuchus	260°	Virgo	210°	Sagittarius	290°	Pisces	30°
February	Sagittarius	290°	Virgo	200°	Capricornus	293°	Pisces	32°
March	Aquarius	330°	Virgo	190°	Capricornus	296°	Cetus	33°
April	Pisces	10°	Leo	170°	Capricornus	299°	Cetus	33°
May	Aries	50°	Leo	160°	Capricornus	302°	Pisces	32°
June	Taurus	80°	Leo	170°	Capricornus	305°	Pisces	31°
July	Cancer	120°	Virgo	190°	Capricornus	308°	Pisces	30°
August	Leo	160°	Virgo	210°	Capricornus	311°	Pisces	29°
September	Virgo	190°	Libra	230°	Capricornus	314°	Pisces	28°
October	Libra	220°	Scorpius	250°	Capricornus	317°	Pisces	27°
November	Sagittarius	260°	Ophiuchus	260°	Capricornus	320°	Pisces	26°
December	Sagittarius	290°	Sagittarius	270°	Capricornus	323°	Pisces	25°

Note: This lesson's concepts will be better understood if the planets are plotted first and the analysis occurs on another day.

Planets on the Move *(cont.)*

Day One Procedure:

1. Explain that students in small groups will plot the locations of four planets on the first day of each month of 1997. Explain the Constellation Chart, pointing out the equator, ecliptic, and constellations. Explain that scientists today use two more constellations near the ecliptic to fill gaps between some of the zodiac constellations. These two are *Ophiuchus* (o-fee-YOU-kus) and *Cetus* (SEE-tus). Remind them that ancient astronomers noticed that the sun appeared to follow a path, gradually moving eastward day by day. Show them the ecliptic, the sun's path through the zodiac constellations. Explain that if the edges of the chart could be brought together, it would show a continuous chain of constellations like the real sky.

   Point out the degrees on the ecliptic from 0° to 180° and back to 0°. Tell the students that this is the astronomers' way of dividing up the sky, just as we add latitude and longitude to the Earth. It helps us find our way around the sky or earth.

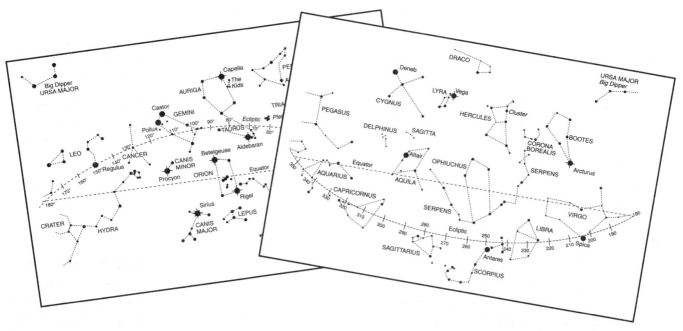

2. Show the transparency of the data and explain that it is very similar to the data Tycho Brahe would have gathered. It shows where the planets will be along the ecliptic for the first of every month of 1997. Tell them they will plot these on the Constellation Chart so they can discover what early astronomers found out about the motion of these planets.

3. Divide the students into eight groups and distribute the data sheets. Demonstrate how the planets should be plotted on the Constellations Chart by having one member of the Venus group plot the January 1 data on the chart. Show how to use the constellation name and degrees to help them find exact location. Place the first initial of each planet's name in pencil on the chart near the correct arc of the ecliptic. Write the number of the month (January = 1) near the initial.

4. Schedule one student from each group to place their data on the chart in order of the dates. (Students should be able to receive assistance as needed.) Each planet should be recorded using pencil. When the planet returns to the same area, show it above or below the first data. (When all planet data have been recorded, the teacher should trace the data in colored ink, using a different color for each planet.)

Planets on the Move *(cont.)*

Day Two Procedure:

1. After all the data has been plotted, ask the following questions so students can understand how the models were created to explain the observed motions of these planets.

   - Where are all the planets located? (*Along the ecliptic; none is in the far north or south.*)

   - Compare the 12 locations of Venus and Saturn during the year. (*Venus moves across the entire ecliptic. Saturn stays within the constellations of Aries and Pisces.*)

   - Explain that Venus is closer to the sun and moves faster than Saturn which is much further from the sun. Saturn, therefore, stays in one constellation for many years while Venus moves across all the zodiac constellations in less than one year.

   - In what direction did the planets generally move during this year? (*eastward*)

   - Did any of the planets ever move westward? (*Mars and Saturn did.*)

2. Show the retrograde loops of Mars and Saturn. Trace these planets' paths with a dotted line from January 1 through December 1. Use the same colored pen used earlier for these planets.

3. Explain that this was confusing to people like Ptolemy and Tycho Brahe who believed that all planets orbited around Earth. Show the drawings of Early Theories of the Planetary System. Explain how the models developed by Ptolemy and Tycho Brahe could demonstrate the backward (retrograde) motion of these planets.

4. Point out Copernicus' model and explain that this is the model we use today with the sun in the center of the planets.

Closure:

1. Distribute a copy of the Mars in Retrograde activity sheet and a ruler to each student. Show the transparency and read the instructions to the students. Trace over the line which connects the Earth #1 with the first dot representing Mars. Point out that the record shows Mars appears to be moving east (E) at this time. Draw a dot at the end of this line to represent Mars and explain that it would look like a star seen among the other stars in the night sky.

2. Trace over the line #2 and put a dot at the end of it. Show how the dot (Mars) moved east from its position last month. Write E on the second line beside month 2.

3. Tell the students to do exactly as you did, using the ruler to trace a straight line over positions #1 and #2, then writing the direction on the record. Explain that they should continue to connect the Earth-Mars positions, recording which way the line is pointing after drawing it.

4. When students are finished, show them the transparency of the answer to the activity sheet. Help them understand that since Earth travels faster than Mars in its orbit, it overtakes the planet and passes it just like cars on the freeway. This makes the planet appear to move backwards until Earth continues in its orbit and Mars appears to move ahead again.

Planets on the Move (cont.)

Planet Data

To the Teacher: This data should be distributed among the eight groups of students. Each group will plot six months of data for their planet on the Constellation Chart. They should look for the constellation and then locate the degrees on the ecliptic. The first initial of the planet (e.g., V = Venus) and number of the month (e.g., January = 1) should be placed near the correct area. When two planets are in the same location, put their data close together without superimposing them. The data may be placed above or below the ecliptic but should appear close to it.

	Venus Constellation		Mars Constellation		Jupiter Constellation		Saturn Constellation	
Month								
January	Ophiuchus	260°	Virgo	210°	Sagittarius	290°	Pisces	30°
February	Sagittarius	290°	Virgo	200°	Capricornus	293°	Pisces	32°
March	Aquarius	330°	Virgo	190°	Capricornus	296°	Cetus	33°
April	Pisces	10°	Leo	170°	Capricornus	299°	Cetus	33°
May	Aries	50°	Leo	160°	Capricornus	302°	Pisces	32°
June	Taurus	80°	Leo	170°	Capricornus	305°	Pisces	31°
July	Cancer	120°	Virgo	190°	Capricornus	308°	Pisces	30°
August	Leo	160°	Virgo	210°	Capricornus	311°	Pisces	29°
September	Virgo	190°	Libra	230°	Capricornus	314°	Pisces	28°
October	Libra	220°	Scorpius	250°	Capricornus	317°	Pisces	27°
November	Sagittarius	260°	Ophiuchus	260°	Capricornus	320°	Pisces	26°
December	Sagittarius	290°	Sagittarius	270°	Capricornus	323°	Pisces	25°

1997 Planet Data for First of Each Month

Note: This information was derived from the following Web site address: *www.astro.wisc.edu/"dolan/Planets-const.cig?years=1997.* Information for planet locations from 1900 to 2000 can be reached through this site as well.

Constellation Chart (Part 1)

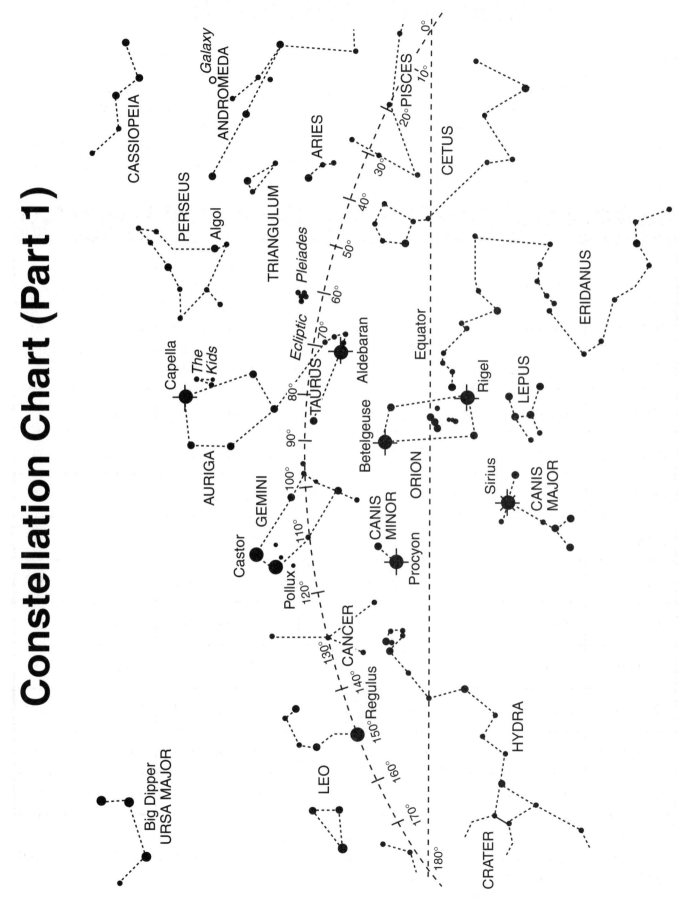

Constellation Chart (Part 2)

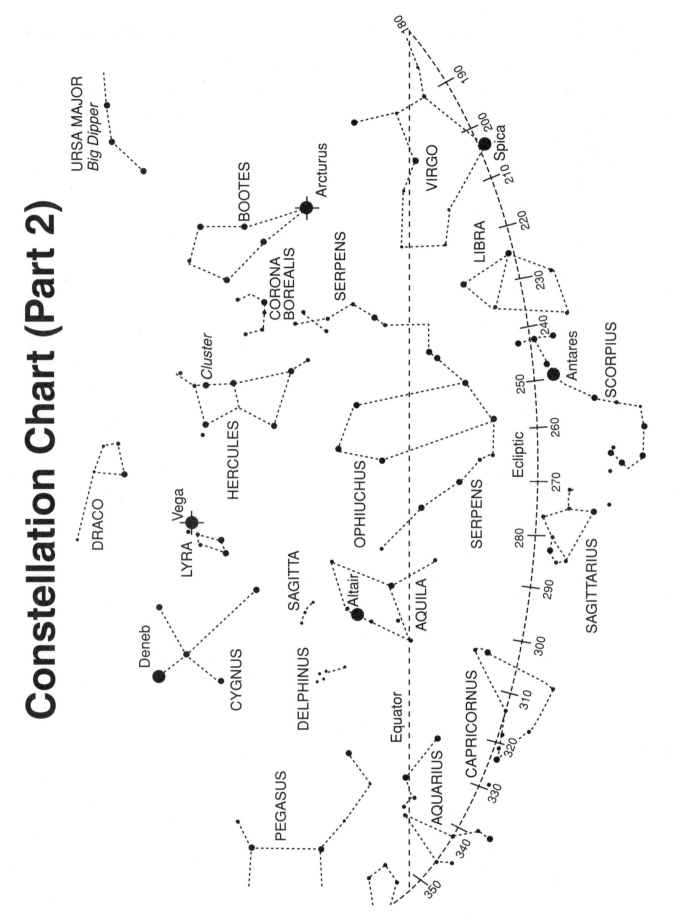

Early Theories of the Planetary System

Ptolemy's Model of Planets—A.D. 150

This diagram shows only two planets as examples from Ptolemy's model. His model showed all the planets out to Saturn, orbiting in a small circle, whose center orbited in a larger circle around Earth. It did explain how these planets would sometimes appear to move backwards (retrograde) against the stars, as seen from Earth.

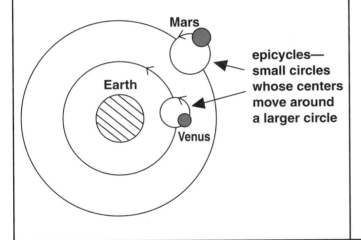

Copernican Model of Planets—1543

Copernicus believed that the sun was in the center of all the planets, although he could not prove his theory. Using a telescope, Galileo was able to show Copernicus' theory was correct in 1610.

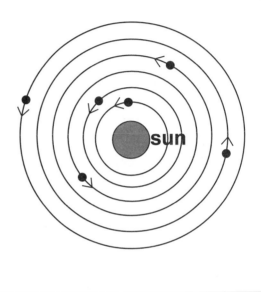

Tycho Brahe's Model of Planets—1588

Tycho Brahe could not find any proof that Earth was moving, so his planetary model shows Earth in a fixed position with the moon orbiting it. He thought the planets orbited the sun, but the sun and these planets orbited Earth. This model was never worked out in mathematical detail but did preserve some of the Copernican system and the spirit of the Ptolemaic system. It also demonstrated how planets would appear to retrograde from Earth as they moved around the sun.

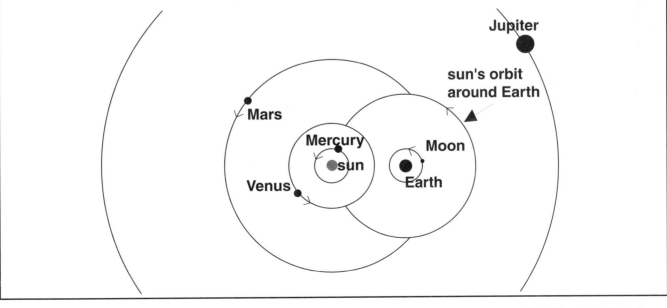

Mars in Retrograde

To the Student: Pretend you are out in space, looking down on the orbits of Earth and Mars. You are able to watch these planets move in their orbits around the sun for nine months. Each dot on the orbits represents the position of that planet during one month. Connect the planets with a straight line and project the line into space to see how it would appear if you were standing on Earth looking at Mars against the stars in space. The first two months have been done as an example of how long the lines should be. Watch as you connect the dots to see which way the line points. Mark the direction Mars appears to move against the stars—east, west, or standing still.

E ⟷ **W**

Month	Direction
1	E
2	E
3	____
4	____
5	____
6	____
7	____
8	____
9	____

Mars' Orbit

SUN

Earth's Orbit

Mars in Retrograde Answers

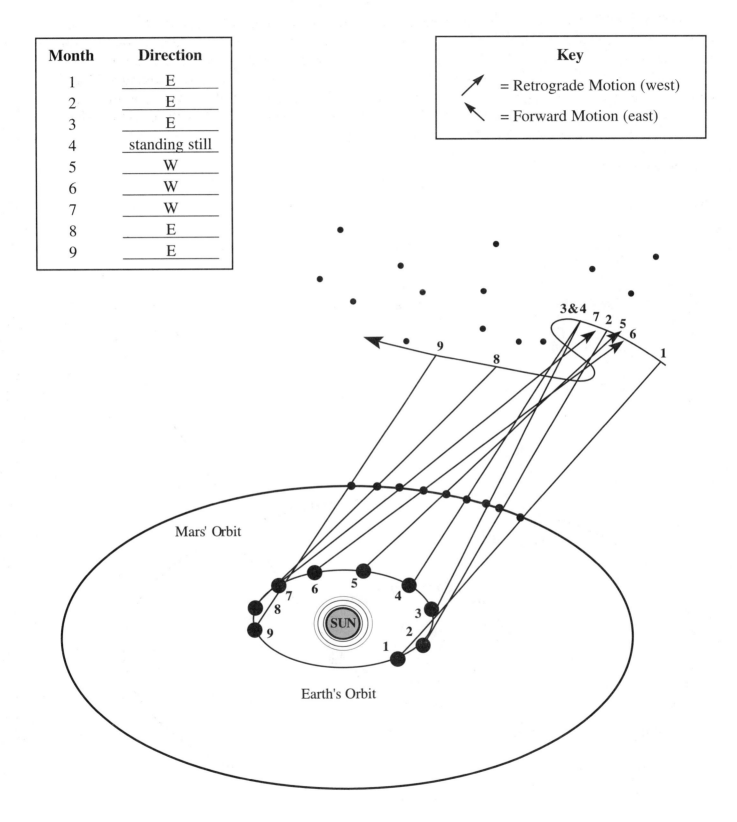

Month	Direction
1	E
2	E
3	E
4	standing still
5	W
6	W
7	W
8	E
9	E

Key

↗ = Retrograde Motion (west)

↖ = Forward Motion (east)

Mars' Orbit

Earth's Orbit

SUN

By the Moons of Jupiter

Teacher Information: When Galileo Galilei pointed his homemade telescope at the moon, sun, planets, and Milky Way, he could see things invisible to the naked eye. Most people of his time believed that the moon, sun, and planets were smooth spheres revolving around the earth. Through his telescope, Galileo could see the moon was pockmarked with craters and had mountains on it. He also pointed the telescope at the planets and discovered that Jupiter had four moons. After observing these for several nights, he concluded they were orbiting the planet. Thus, the accepted theory of his day that everything orbited Earth was proven wrong.

Materials: 12 file cards 3" x 5" (8 cm x 13 cm) and a copy of the Flipbook of Jupiter's Moons (page 29) for each student; scissors; glue; wide, clear packing tape

Procedure:

1. Distribute 12 file cards and a copy of page 29 to each student. Tell them to carefully cut out each picture. Show them how to glue each picture to the lower left corner of a card. Place the cards in order with #1 on top.

2. Stack the cards so the edges are offset about ¼ inch (.6 cm). On the back of the cards, use clear packing tape across the top edges both vertically and horizontally to hold the cards in place.

3. Have students flip through the book to see Jupiter's moons move back and forth on either side of the planet, sometimes passing in front (#5, #6, #7, and #12).

a. single card b. two cards

c. stacked cards d. flipbook

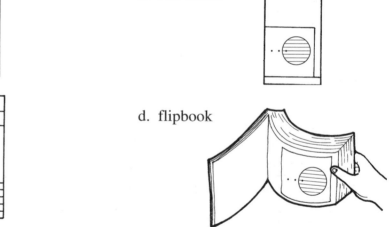

4. Explain that as Galileo made drawings of these moons each evening, he noticed they changed positions on either side of Jupiter. He concluded they were in orbit around the planet. This would make them appear at times on one side, then the other, even passing in front of the planet.

5. Tell students today these moons are called the *Galilean moons,* and we use the names Galileo gave to them.

6. Write on the board the names of the moons and the number of days each takes to orbit Jupiter.

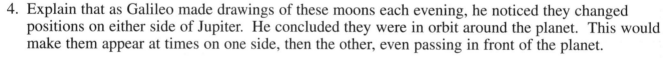

Io—1.77 days	*Ganymede*—7.166 days
Europa—3.55 days	*Callisto*—16.75 days

Closure:

Ask students which of these moons is the most distant from Jupiter and how they know. (*Callisto*—it takes the longest time to complete its orbit.) Have them tell you which moon is closest and how they know this. (*Io*—it moves the fastest around the planet.)

By the Moons of Jupiter *(cont.)*

Flipbook of Jupiter's Moons

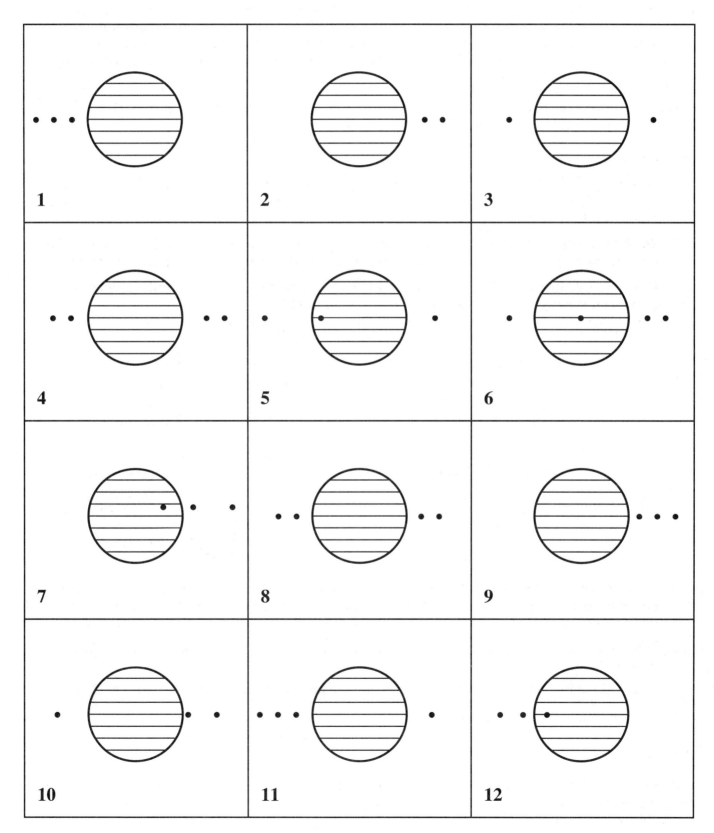

We Become Space Travelers

Summary

This chapter covers the history of the exciting, manned-space exploration era, beginning with the launch of Sputnik by the Union of Soviet Socialist Republics (USSR) in 1957, through the Mercury, Gemini, Apollo, and space shuttle missions. It ends with the International Space Station (ISS), scheduled to be constructed over the next five years as a joint venture with 16 stations.

Overview of Activities

A variety of multidisciplinary activities develop the students' understanding of the history of our efforts to reach beyond the boundaries of our own planet. These include creating a time line of the history of the space race between the US and USSR to be the first to set a person on the moon. The sizes of the US and USSR spacecrafts used during these efforts are compared. The six Apollo landing sites are plotted on a moon map. A simulation of how the moon's phases occur helps students understand why the moon changes its shape everyday. A demonstration to show the moon's rotation around its axis explains why the astronauts landed only on one side of the moon. Students make a drawing of how the moon looks from Earth and how the Earth appeared to the Apollo 11 crew while they were at the moon. The dimensions of the first US space station, Skylab, are laid out so that students will gain an understanding of how the space race changed into a cooperative venture; the Apollo/Soyuz mission between the US and USSR as well as the recent visits to the Russian Mir space station are studied. Students design an activity the crews of Apollo and Soyuz could do in order to become familiar with each other while in space. Sitting within the area of the space shuttle's mid-deck living quarters section helps students understand how small this is. It is then compared to the spacious International Space Station (ISS), which some of the students may visit one day. They write an illustrated story telling what it would be like to be a member of the scientific research team on the ISS.

Setting the Stage

Conduct the activities in The Great Space Race chapter in which students become teams who represent the US and USSR in a race to be the first to land on the moon. This will help them develop a historical perspective of the space programs in the years from 1957 through 1972.

Supplemental Materials

A variety of books, Internet Web sites, videotapes, and other materials related to this chapter are described in the annotated Resources section at the end of this book.

Extending This Chapter

This chapter is extended by continuing on to the one which follows it, Touring the Solar System. Many of the students will have the opportunity to become a part of future space adventures. These two chapters will show why it is so important to continue the effort to explore space.

The Great Space Race

Teacher Information: German scientists developed the V2 rocket during the latter part of World War II. This powerful rocket was capable of sending an armed missile across a great distance without the use of aircraft. Following World War II, both the US and USSR brought some of these rocket scientists out of Germany and sent them to work in science labs with scientists from those nations. Their objective was to build rockets capable of carrying a vehicle into space. The launch of Sputnik by the USSR on October 4, 1957, was a complete surprise to the USA since all launches done by the Soviet Union were done in secret. It was labeled the Second Moon since it orbited the Earth about once every 90 minutes. It appeared as a faint star crossing the night sky west to east. This was a huge blow to Americans because a communist country had beaten them into space. The second surprise came a month later when Sputnik II was launched, this time with the dog Laika aboard. This put the space race into high gear as the US and USSR began to build bigger and better launch vehicles. The winner was the first nation to place a person on the moon.

Materials: transparency of The Great Space Race scoreboard (page 32), overhead projector, large sheet of butcher paper, red and blue markers, History of the Space Race cards (page 33), 2.4-inch (6 cm) wide adding-machine tape (*Optional:* Apollo II video and pictures of manned space flight [See Resources section.])

Lesson Preparation:

1. Copy the History of the Space Race cards onto cardstock and cut them into individual cards.
2. Follow the directions on The Great Space Race scoreboard to transfer it onto large paper.
3. Cut 16 feet (5 m) of the tape and divide it into one-foot (30 cm) sections. Mark each section with a different year from 1957 through 1972. Post this strip on a blank bulletin board to serve as a basis of a time line showing the history of space exploration during these years.
4. You may wish to add to the excitement of this race by having the students make paper flags for their US and USSR teams to wave every time they score a point.

Procedure:

1. Tell the students about the beginning of the space race from the Teacher Information above.
2. Explain that they are going to play a game which will show them how this race unfolded after Sputnik I and II were launched.
3. Post the scoreboard sheet in the front of the class. Divide the students into two teams, one for the US and the other for the USSR. Distribute the 16 race cards to individual students.
4. Assign a scorekeeper for each team to be stationed near the scoreboard. Give a blue marker to the US scorekeeper and a red marker to the USSR recorder.
5. Explain that the race cards should be read aloud as you call out their year. As the information is read, the scorekeepers should mark a slash(/) for the nation which accomplished the goal. When four slash marks have been made, the fifth should be drawn through them to make a set of five ||||, thus it will be easier to total the score.
6. After each card is read, post it along the time line near the proper date.
7. Show the score for each nation for each year, accumulating points from previous years.
8. Announce the winner after 1969 (US) but continue to keep score until 1972 when the Apollo missions ended.

Closure:

1. Have the students discuss how each nation must have felt as they succeeded or failed in their attempts to attain the goals they had set.
2. Show a video of Mercury and Gemini launches and the Apollo 11 landing on the moon.

The Great Space Race *(cont.)*

To the Teacher: Use a transparency of this chart to enlarge and then trace it with pencil onto the butcher paper. Use colored pens to enhance the drawing. Color the flags with appropriate colors. The USSR flag is red with a gold hammer, sickle, and star on it. (**Note:** This is not the Russian flag in use today.)

The Great Space Race Scoreboard					
Year	🇺🇸	**US**	☐	☭	**USSR**	☐
1957		☐			☐
1958		☐			☐
1959		☐			☐
1960		☐			☐
1961		☐			☐
1962		☐			☐
1963		☐			☐
1964		☐			☐
1965		☐			☐
1966		☐			☐
1967		☐			☐
1968		☐			☐
1969		☐			☐
And the winner is. . . .					
1970		☐			☐
1971		☐			☐
1972		☐			☐

History of the Space Race

1957

Sputnik I (USSR)—First satellite to orbit Earth.

Sputnik II (USSR)—First orbiting life form, a dog named Laika.

1958

Explorer I (US)—First American satellite, unmanned.

Vanguard (US)—First solar-powered satellite.

Sputnik III (USSR)—First data about Earth taken from orbit.

1959

Luna I (USSR)—First spacecraft to travel beyond Earth orbit. Missed the moon and went into orbit around the sun.

Pioneer 4 (US)—First American deep-space probe passed within 37,300 miles of moon and then into solar orbit.

Jupiter (US)—First primates (two chimpanzees) launched into partial orbit around Earth.

Explorer 6 (US)—First photo of Earth from space.

Luna 2 (USSR)—First lunar probe to impact on moon.

Luna 3 (USSR)—First lunar probe to photograph moon's far side (which is never seen from Earth.)

1960

Echo I (US)—First passive (reflector) communications satellite.

Sputnik V (USSR)—First recovery of orbited animals from space (two dogs).

Courier 18 (US)—First active repeater communication satellite.

1961

Mercury 2 (US)—First test of *Mercury-Redstone* flight vehicle with a chimpanzee. Partial orbit of Earth.

Venera (USSR)—Venus probe, passed within 62,000 miles of Venus.

Vostok 1 (USSR)—First manned space flight, Yuri Gagarin. One orbit of Earth.

Mercury-Freedom 7 (US)—Alan Shepard, first American in space. Partial orbit of Earth.

Mercury 4 (US)—Gus Grissom, partial orbit. Capsule sank on return but astronaut rescued.

Vostok 2 (USSR)—Manned space flight by Gherman Titov. Traveled 16 times around the Earth in 25 hours.

Mercury 5 (US)—First US live orbital flight of chimpanzee. Recovered after two orbits.

1962

Mercury-Friendship (US)—First US manned orbital flight. John Glenn makes three orbits around the Earth.

Ranger 4 (US)—First American lunar probe to impact on moon. No data since camera failed.

Mercury 7 (US)—Scott Carpenter makes three orbits around Earth.

Vostok 3 (USSR)—Part of Soviet dual mission (with *Vostok 4*). Orbited 3 days, 22 hours.

Vostok 4 (USSR)—Part of first Soviet dual mission. Came within 3.1 miles of *Vostok 3*. Orbited 2 days, 23 hours.

Mariner 2 (US)—First successful flyby of Venus.

Mercury 8 (US)—Walter Schirra, six orbits around Earth.

1963

Mercury 9 (US)—First American-manned flight over 24 hours.

Vostok 5 (USSR)—Part of dual mission (with *Vostok 6*), 81 orbits.

Vostok 6 (USSR)—Dual mission, came within three miles of *Vostok 5*. 48 orbits.

History of the Space Race *(cont.)*

1964

Ranger 7 (US)—First successful American lunar probe; returned 4,316 closeup photos of moon's surface before impacting moon.

Voshkod 1 (USSR)—First three-man mission to orbit Earth, 16 orbits.

Mariner 4 (US)—First successful flyby of Mars.

1966

Luna 9 (USSR)—First soft landing on moon, returned surface photos of the moon.

Gemini 8 (US)—First meeting in space with previously launched target (*Agena 11*). This was practice for later flights to the moon. Astronaut Neil Armstrong stopped the spin. Mission ended early.

Luna 10 (USSR)—First lunar orbiter, returned moon data until May 1966.

Surveyor 1 (US)—First American soft landing on moon, returned 11,240 photos.

Gemini 9 (US)—Linked to *Agena*, unmanned spacecraft. Spacewalk of 2 hours, 8 minutes by astronaut Eugene Cernan.

Gemini 10 (US)—First use of target vehicle as source of propulsion after meeting and docking in space; first double meeting in space (*Agena 8* and *10*); first retrieval of space object (test package of target vehicle).

Luna Orbiter 1 (US)—Orbited moon and returned 297 photos of moon equatorial region, searching for landing sites. (**Note:** All orbiters were sent crashing into the moon so their radio transmissions would not interfere with later spacecraft.)

Gemini 11 (US)—Met and docked with *Agena 11*. Flew at a record altitude of 850 miles above the Earth.

Gemini 12 (US)—Final mission for Gemini program. Three spacewalks for total of 5 hours, 30 minutes, a new record.

1965

Voshod II (USSR)—First space walk (10 minutes). Cosmonaut Leonov's space suit expanded when heated by the sun and needed to be deflated somewhat before he could get back inside the space vehicle.

Gemini 3 (US)—First two-man crew to orbit, and first time people got to control the maneuvers in space.

Gemini 4 (US)—First American space walk (21 minutes).

Proton 1 (USSR)—Physics lab in space.

Gemini 5 (US)—First extended manned flight of 128 orbits.

Venera 3 (USSR)—Impacted Venus on March 1, 1966; no data.

Gemini 6 and **Gemini 7** (US)—First meeting of spacecraft while in orbit.

1967

Apollo 1 (US)—Fire inside the spacecraft during ground testing resulted in death of three astronauts.

Soyuz 1 (USSR)—First manned test flight of new Soviet spacecraft. All Soviet spacecrafts landed on ground; the US spacecrafts landed in the ocean and were picked up by a ship. The cosmonaut on this flight was killed when his parachute failed during reentry and he crashed into the ground.

Surveyor 3 (US)—Landed on moon. Took photos and did a soil analysis.

Venera 4 (USSR)—First successful probe of Venus's atmosphere.

Luna Orbiter 5 (US)—Photos of five possible landing sites.

Surveyor 6 (US)—Performed first rocket liftoff from moon, practicing for future manned moon missions.

Apollo 4 (US)—First successful unmanned Apollo flight to test the system which would take men to the moon.

History of the Space Race *(cont.)*

1968

Apollo 5 (US)—First flight of lunar module (unmanned).

Zond 5 (USSR)—First satellite to fly around moon and return to Earth.

Apollo 7 (US)—First American three-man Earth orbital mission.

Soyuz 2 (USSR)—Unmanned satellite; met target in orbit.

Soyuz 3 (USSR)—Manned spacecraft moved to within 650 feet of *Soyuz 2.*

Zond 6 (USSR)—Flew around moon and then returned to Earth, landing in the USSR.

Apollo 8 (US)—First manned orbit of moon, three astronauts.

1969

Soyuz 4 (USSR)—First docking (with *Soyuz 5*) of two manned Soviet spacecraft.

Soyuz 5 (USSR)—Docked with *Soyuz 4.*

Mariner 6 (US)—Flew by Mars, transmitting 75 pictures.

Apollo 9 (US)—First test of lunar module in Earth orbit, three astronauts on board.

Apollo 10 (US)—First test of lunar module while orbiting the moon, three astronauts on board.

Apollo 11 (US)—**First manned lunar landing. First men on the moon: Neil Armstrong and Buzz Aldrin. Michael Collins remained in orbit around the moon in the command module, 22 hours on the moon.**

Soyuz 6, 7 and *8* (USSR)—First triple launch, non-docking group flight.

Apollo 12 (US)—Second manned lunar landing, returned parts from *Surveyor 3*, US unmanned lander sent in 1967, 32 hours on the moon.

1970

Apollo 13 (US)—Third manned lunar landing attempt, aborted due to oxygen tank explosion in service module. All three crew members returned to Earth safely.

Soyuz 9 (USSR)—Set new duration record for manned space flight time at 17 days, 17 hours, and 59 minutes.

Luna 16 (USSR)—First unmanned lunar rover landed on moon.

Venera 7 (USSR)—Probe into Venus's atmosphere, first successful (unmanned) landing on Venus.

1971

Apollo 14 (US)—Third manned lunar landing, collected 96 pounds of lunar specimens, 34 hours on the moon.

Salyut 1 (USSR)—First orbiting space station and lab.

Soyuz 10 (USSR)—First crew to dock with orbiting *Salyut 1* space station.

Mars 2 (US)—First vehicle to land on Mars.

Mariner 9 (US)—First successful Mars orbiter, returned 7,000 pictures of surface.

Soyuz 11 (USSR)—First crew to occupy *Salyut 1* space station (24 days). When the spacecraft carrying three cosmonauts pulled away from the space station, an air leak occurred. Their spacecraft returned safely to Earth, but the crew was found dead.

Apollo 15 (US)—Fourth manned lunar landing, first use of lunar rover, 67 hours on the moon.

1972

Pioneer 10 (US)—First successful flyby of Jupiter. Years later it was the first probe to escape solar system.

Venera 8 (USSR)—Landed on Venus and lasted long enough to transmit surface data.

Apollo 16 (US)—Fifth manned lunar landing, collected 213 pounds of samples, used a lunar rover, 71 hours on the moon.

ERT 1 (US)—First Earth satellite to gather data about our planet.

Apollo 17 (US)—Sixth and last lunar landing, collected 243 pounds of samples, used the lunar rover, 76 hours on the moon.

Early Space Vehicles

Teacher Information: The Soviet Union and United States needed large rockets to carry people into space. Many of these originated from those used as war rockets. The USSR was capable of building larger rockets before the US developed the Saturn rocket, which ultimately carried men to the moon.

Materials: at least 320 yards (291 m) of heavy string, 5 pieces of 5" x 5" (13 cm x 13 cm) of heavy cardboard, 5 metal washers (*Optional:* pictures of the five space vehicles [See Resources section.])

Lesson Preparation:

1. Prepare the cards by labeling each with the name of one of the space vehicles. Put the length and nation who owned each spacecraft on the cards as well. Laminate them for strength, and punch a hole in the center of one side.

2. Cut the string to the lengths shown on the chart below and attach the pieces to the respective card. Wrap the string around the card and then attach a washer to the end to prevent unraveling.

Space Vehicles Used by the United States and Union of Soviet Socialist Republics

Name/Nation	Length	Years	Missions
Vostok/USSR	125 ft. (38 m)	1957–1964	Launched Sputnik I and II and cosmonauts, including Yuri Gagarin, first man in space.
Mercury/US	87 ft. (26 m)	1962–1963	Carried one astronaut. Alan Shepard was first American to orbit the Earth.
Gemini/US	160 ft. (48 m)	1965–1967	Carried two astronauts. Practiced docking in space in preparation for missions to the moon.
Soyuz/USSR	167 ft. (50 m)	1967–(?)	Manned launches of two cosmonauts. Practiced dockings in preparation for missions to the moon. Later used to carry men to Earth-orbiting space station.
Apollo on Saturn Rocket/US	363 ft. (109 m)	1967–1975	Carried three astronauts. Used for six landings on the moon carrying three crew members and lunar lander.

Procedure:

Take students to a large field and select 10 students to work in pairs. They will stretch out the strings, one vehicle at a time, in the order shown in the chart. Lay the strings on the ground.

Closure:

Have students walk the lengths of the strings to compare their sizes. Be sure they see the evolution that took place over the years. Show photographs of spacecrafts.

Apollo Landing Sites

Teacher Information: There were six Apollo missions that carried astronauts to the moon. Each had three crew members on board, but only two members of each crew actually landed on the moon. The third remained in the command module which orbited the moon during the landing. This makes a total of only 12 men who have walked on the moon. Now that students have done The Great Space Race activity, this lesson will summarize the landings.

Materials: copies of Plotting the Apollo Landing Sites data sheet for each student, map of the moon, six flags (below), pins (*Optional:* video on the lunar landings from NASA)

National Geographic has an excellent moon map; see the Resources section of this book for further information on ordering it.

Lesson Preparation:

Cut out the six Apollo landing flags below, and mount each on a pin. Post the lunar map on a bulletin board.

Procedure:

1. Remind the students of The Great Space Race information by referring to the time line they completed as they kept score for the two nations involved in the race. Briefly discuss the Apollo missions.

2. Distribute a copy of Plotting the Apollo Landing Sites to each student and review the directions with them. Show them the location of the Apollo 11 landing site marked on the moon and show them how to use the latitude and longitude coordinates to locate this site.

Closure:

Have students pin the flags on the moon landing sites. Review the History of the Space Race cards to explain why Apollo 13 is missing from the missions which landed.

Discuss the locations of these sites. Ask students what part of the moon was favored for landing locations. (The landing sites are concentrated around the equator.)

Point out that all landing sites are on the same side of the moon. Explain that we only see one side of the moon from Earth. Tell them that you are going to be the moon and they are on Earth watching you. Walk around the room, always facing the students. Tell them that you are rotating around your axis at the same time you are orbiting the Earth and thus always keeping your face to them. Show what would happen if you did not rotate by pointing your face in one direction and walking around the students. They will then see all parts of you. Explain that the landing sties were on the side of the moon which always faces the Earth so that the astronauts would be able to communicate with people on Earth at Mission Control.

Apollo 11, July 1969 1° N lat. 24° E long.	Apollo 12, Nov. 1969 3° S lat. 23° W long.	Apollo 14, Jan. 1971 4° S lat. 18° W long.
Apollo 15, July 1971 26° N lat. 4° E long.	Apollo 16, April 1972 9° S lat. 16° E long.	Apollo 17, Dec. 1972 20° N lat. 30° E long.

Plotting the Apollo Landing Sites

Directions: Use the chart below to plot the landing sites of the six Apollo missions.

1. Start at the 0° point on the moon map and move north or south to find the latitude.
2. Begin again in the center at 0° and move east or west to find the longitude.
3. Put the letter of the Apollo mission on the spot where the latitude and longitude meet.

The Apollo 11 landing site is shown on the moon map to help you.

	Mission	Latitude	Longitude	Area	Date
	Apollo Landing Sites				
A	Apollo 11	1° north	24° east	Sea of Tranquility	July 1969
B	Apollo 12	3° south	23° west	Ocean of Storms	November 1969
C	Apollo 14	4° south	18° west	Fra Mauro	January 1971
D	Apollo 15	26° north	4° east	Hadley-Apennine	July 1971
E	Apollo 16	9° south	16° east	Descartes	April 1972
F	Apollo 17	20° north	30° east	Taulus-Littrow	December 1972

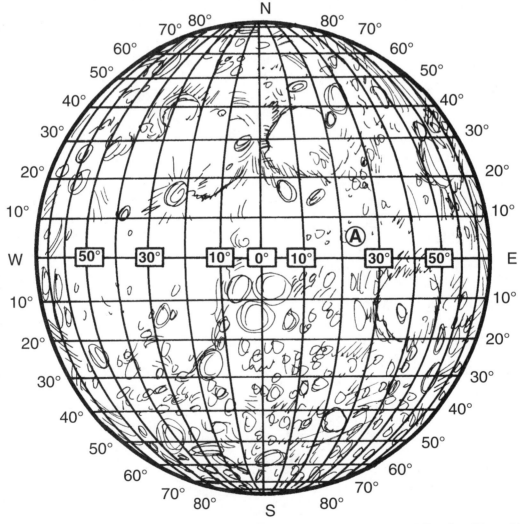

The Moon's Phases

Teacher Information: Engage students in a month-long study of moon phases. Begin the activity when the moon is one day past new, checking a newspaper or calendar for current moon phases.

Materials: 2" (5 cm) Styrofoam ball glued to a stick for each student and teacher, clamp-on light fixture with 150-watt bulb, transparency of The Moon's Phases chart (page 40), parent letter

Lesson Preparation:

1. Push the stick halfway into the center of the Styrofoam ball. Remove it, pour white glue into the hole, and reinsert the stick. Let these dry for a day before using them.
2. Place the clamp-on light high on a wall in a darkened room.

Procedure:

1. Ask students to draw moon shapes they have seen. Let them write brief, illustrated explanations for how the moon changes its shape.
2. Give each student a Styrofoam ball. It will represent the moon, they will be the Earth, and the light will be the sun.
3. Spread students across the room and turn out the lights. Show how to simulate the moon's motion. Holding the moon between your face and the light, show that the side of the moon facing you gets no sunlight. Let students do this with their moons.
4. Turn slowly counterclockwise, holding the moon in front of your face. Let students do the same and tell them to watch the light on the moon as they turn. (The light on the ball appears as a thin crescent on the right side.)
5. Tell students to continue to slowly rotate, keeping the moon in front of their faces, high enough so that shadow falls on it. Have them keep up with your position. Describe what they should be seeing. (*More light falls on the right side of the moon until one side is fully illuminated—a full moon.*)
6. As they continue to rotate, point out that the right side of the moon begins to darken and light falls on the left side. Rotate to the beginning position, facing the sun.
7. Repeat the rotation and introduce names of the phases. When moon, sun, and Earth are lined up, no light shines on the side of the moon we face (new phase). Following that is the thin crescent, the first quarter, the gibbous moon, and, finally, the full moon when the sun is on one side of Earth and the moon on the other. Have students notice where the sun is during all phases.
8. Have them continue to rotate so they can see the phases in reverse after they pass the full moon. Name these phases: gibbous, last quarter, crescent. Tell students to rotate slowly several times and watch to see the phases change.

Closure:

- Show the transparency of The Moon's Phases and point out how the sun illuminates the moon, just as it did in the simulation.
- Have students begin to watch the moon each evening, beginning when the moon is a few days past new. Have them bring in a drawing to show how it changes each day and post these on the bulletin board.
- Look for the moon in the daytime sky east of the sun after the first quarter and then west of the sun after. Have the students go outside to see these phases and discuss how they compare to their simulation.

The Moon's Phases *(cont.)*

Compare the phases of the moon shown on this chart with those you saw in the simulation.

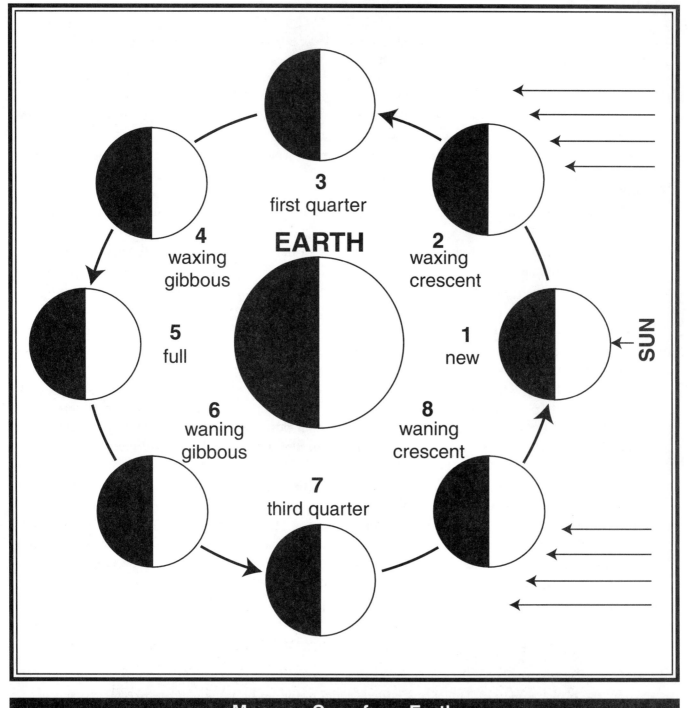

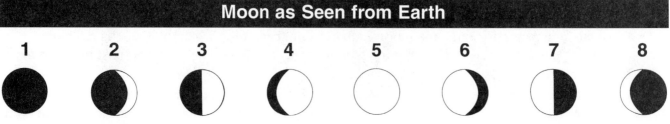

40

Cosmic Art

New Horizons

This is an exercise in imagining a different perspective. Your students will be challenged to imagine they are aboard Apollo 11 and will draw what Earth looks like from the moon.

1. Tell students they are going on an imaginary journey to the moon with the crew of *Apollo 11*. After launch on July 16, 1969, they will orbit Earth. While in orbit, they will draw a view of the moon. After arriving at the moon on July 20, they will make another drawing of what Earth looks like from the moon.

2. Distribute to each student a piece of 17" x 22" (43 cm x 56 cm) black drawing paper to represent space, which is black since there is no atmosphere to scatter light and make a blue sky as we see it on Earth. Have them fold this paper in half.

3. Give the students a pencil compass and a piece of blue paper the size of one side of the folded black paper. Show them photos taken by the Apollo 11 crew (see Resources section). Explain that the astronauts orbited so near Earth they could see only part of it. Tell students to draw a quarter arc at the bottom of the narrow edge of blue paper. Within this arc, they should draw the upper part of the North American continent. Glue cotton over areas of Earth to represent clouds. Have them cut out the Earth picture and paste it at the bottom of the black paper.

4. The moon should be a circle no larger than a dime, cut from white paper. Students should cut the circle into a crescent to represent a five-day-old moon. (See # 2 on The Moon's Phases.) Paste it above Earth on their pictures. Be sure they show the moon with the right side illuminated.

5. Distribute a piece of gray paper on which students can draw an arc at the narrow edge to represent the moon. Show them a picture of the moon and Earth as seen by *Apollo 11* astronauts by using Internet or NASA information. (See Resources section.) Explain that the astronauts orbited close to the moon, so they saw only a part of it. The moon appeared gray to them when they got close. Let students draw craters on their moon pictures.

6. Have them draw another circle on blue paper to represent Earth as seen from the moon. This circle should be the diameter of a quarter and cut in the shape of a waning gibbous moon. (See # 6 on The Moon's Phases.) Have them draw Africa on it and cover parts of Earth with white cotton clouds. (**Note:** Apollo 11 photos show Earth tilted so Africa appears lying on its side, due to the camera angle.)

7. Visit the Web site for phases of the moon (see Resources) to find out the exact phase as seen from Earth on July 20, 1969.

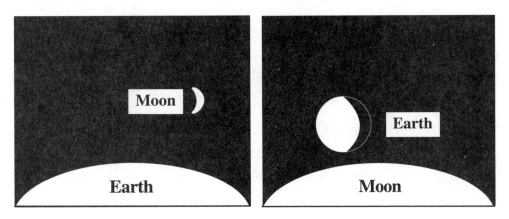

Skylab

Teacher Information: Skylab, the first American space station, was launched in 1973. It was constructed inside the second stage of a three-stage Saturn rocket, which had lifted the Apollo spacecraft into space. During launch, a solar panel and the meteoroid shield were torn off. The first crew of three astronauts were launched a few days later to Skylab and fastened an umbrella made of thin, reflective mylar to the side of the space station. Skylab now began to cool off. They also were able to release the solar panel, and when it opened, it began to generate the electrical power needed on the space station.

Skylab was visited by three crews of three astronauts during 1973. The longest stay on board was 84 days. The space station was large enough for the astronauts to move around in comfortably. Since it was pressurized like an airplane, they didn't have to wear space suits unless they had to go outside. The crew did many research projects, including using a telescope to observe and photograph the sun and Comet Kohoutek. They also photographed Earth and showed views of land formations, ocean currents, and the atmosphere.

At the end of the last trip to Skylab in 1973, the space station was positioned into a stable attitude, and systems were shut down. It was expected that Skylab would remain in orbit eight to 10 years. However, in the fall of 1977, it was determined that Skylab was gradually slowing in orbit as a result of more than usual solar radiation which made the atmosphere swell. This created a drag on the space station, slowing it and dropping it into ever lower orbit. Finally, it fell back to Earth on July 11, 1979. Most of the space station burned up in the atmosphere; the rest of the debris spread over an area from the southeastern Indian Ocean across a sparsely populated section of western Australia. The people in Perth, Australia, saw a spectacular fireworks display. No one was hurt, but several large pieces of Skylab were found in a remote area of Australia.

Materials: 50 yards (45 m) of heavy string, transparency of Skylab, NASA video *Four Rooms, Earth View* (See Resources for NASA order information.)

Lesson Preparation:

Use the dimensions shown with the Skylab pictures to cut strings to represent the length and diameter of the space station.

Procedure:

1. Show a transparency of Skylab and share the information regarding this space station.
2. Take the students to a large field and stretch out the strings to show them the length and diameter of Skylab.

Closure:

- Compare this to the 363-feet (109 m) length of the Apollo/Saturn strings used in the Early Space Vehicles activity (page 36).
- Show the video *Four Rooms, Earth View* which provides a tour of Skylab.

Extender:

If Internet access is available, visit the following Web site to see a picture of Skylab. Other Web sites of interest are listed in the Resources section of this book.

Skylab Images: http://heasarc.gsfc.nasa.gov/Images/pretty_pictures_skylab.html

Skylab *(cont.)*

Length = 119 feet (36 meters)
Diameter = 27 feet (8 meters)
Interior = 12,000 cubic feet (360 cubic meters)

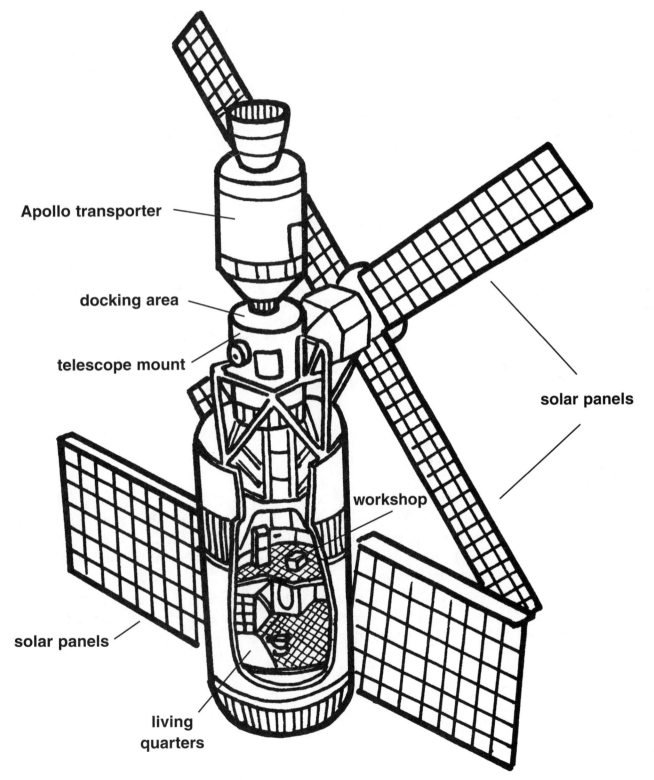

Apollo transporter

docking area

telescope mount

solar panels

workshop

solar panels

living quarters

Comrades in Space

Teacher Information: The first efforts for cooperative space ventures between the US and USSR came in 1975 when the US Apollo and USSR Soyuz spacecrafts linked while in Earth orbit. Three astronauts and two cosmonauts remained docked for two days, exchanging gifts, eating meals together, and signing certificates to commemorate this event. Landing for the cosmonauts was normal, but the three astronauts were nearly killed when their capsule was filled with a yellowish, poisonous gas (nitrogen tetroxide) after it landed upside down in the ocean. This was caused by the thruster units which had been accidentally left on after parachute deployment. They were saved by putting on oxygen masks and opening the capsule's hatch. So ended the Apollo missions and the last expendable spacecraft.

Russia began placing space stations in orbit around the Earth in 1971. These were referred to as Salyut and remained in orbit for varying lengths of time. Russia's longest orbiting space station, Mir (meaning *peace*), has been in orbit for over 10 years. The first section of the station was launched on February 19, 1986, following the Challenger explosion of January 28, 1986. Over the 10 years, modules were added to the station to form a total of seven. Mir has a mass of over 100 tons. Its modules are 90 feet (27 m) in diameter and its length is 107 feet (32 m) when either the Soyuz-TM or Progress-M spacecraft is docked. These spacecrafts shuttle the crew members and supplies between Mir and Russia. This provided living and working quarters for cosmonauts. They could orbit Earth for longer periods of time; some cosmonauts were in space for over a year.

A renewed effort to cooperate with Russia in space resulted in the first link of the space shuttle with Mir in June 1995. An astronaut was brought to Mir to join cosmonauts who had arrived earlier from Russia. Thus began a series of US astronauts staying aboard Mir to study the effects on the human body during long space flights. The Mir space station is no longer being used but has laid the groundwork for the International Space Station, which is being built in cooperation with Russia and other nations.

Materials: 200 feet (60 m) of heavy string, transparency of Apollo/Soyuz spacecraft and Mir space station, *The Illustrated History of NASA* (See Resources section.)

Lesson Preparation:

Cut strings which will equal the length and the diameter of Mir.

Procedure:

1. Provide the students with information regarding the Apollo/Soyuz mission.

2. Have them work in small groups representing the cosmonauts and astronauts who met in space during this mission. Assign them the task of finding more information regarding this mission (see the Web sites in the Resources section.)

3. Explain that this linking of orbiting spacecrafts would be like inviting someone into their home for the first time and trying to make them feel welcome. Have each group describe an activity the two crews could do in order to develop friendly relations.

Closure:

1. Show students pictures of Apollo/Soyuz and Mir. Share the information about the Russian space station. (See the Related Web Sites list in the Resources section for Mir space station information.)

2. Take the students to a large, open area to lay out the strings and compare these with the Skylab space station.

Comrades in Space *(cont.)*

Apollo Soyuz

The first mission of Earth-orbiting spacecraft from Russia and the United States took place on July 17–19, 1975. The crew members were US astronauts Thomas Stafford (commander), Donald Slayton, and Vance Brand and USSR cosmonauts Alexei Leonov and Valery Kubasov.

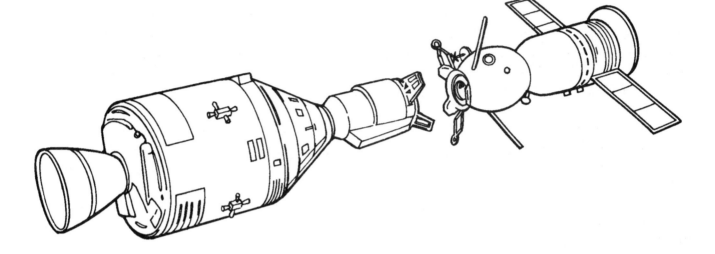

Mir

Mir (meaning *peace*) was launched into space by the USSR on February 19, 1986. It is still orbiting Earth and has had many cosmonauts stay on board. Several were there longer than a year. In 1995, the first US astronauts began to join the Russians aboard Mir to learn how living in space changes the body. This space station is no longer used but is still in orbit.

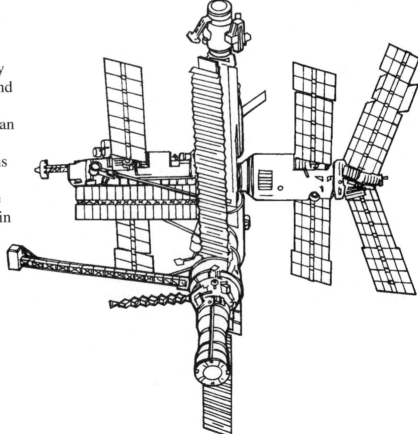

A Magnificent Flying Machine

Teacher Information: The Columbia Space Shuttle was first launched from Kennedy Space Center on April 12, 1981. It was the first US reusable space vehicle that could carry up to a crew of seven into space. There are presently four space shuttles in use—Columbia, Discovery, Atlantis, and Endeavor. The Challenger Space Shuttle was destroyed in an explosion on January 28, 1986, killing its seven crew members, including the first teacher in space, Christa McAuliffe.

The space shuttle program has enabled astronauts to orbit the Earth while conducting many research projects, taking fantastic photographs of Earth and space, as well as launching numerous satellites and the Hubble telescope. It has also served to transport scientists and others to the Russian space station Mir.

Materials: masking tape, 184 feet (56 m) of heavy string, transparency of space shuttle and flight and mid-deck, (*Optional:* space shuttle pictures and video *Space Shuttle Pioneers* [See Resources section.])

Lesson Preparation:

1. Cut a string 184 feet (56 m) long to represent the length of the space shuttle, including the fuel tanks.

2. Clear a space in the classroom, equal to the dimensions of the space shuttle's mid-deck area. Place masking tape on the floor to show the dimensions.

Procedure:

1. Have the students bring their chairs and sit within the area of the space shuttle mid-deck.

2. Show them the transparency of the mid-deck and flight deck. Walk to the areas of the airlock, storage lockers, etc., to show how this makes the living space even smaller.

3. Explain that the ceiling is about 6 feet (1.8 m) high. Tell them that since there is only microgravity in the space shuttle, the crew floats around. This means they are able to use the space above for floor as well so more crew members can fit into the mid-deck.

4. Show the transparency of the space shuttle and tell the information about it.

5. If available, show pictures and a video on the space shuttle history.

Closure:

1. Take the students outside and have them stretch out the length of the space shuttle. Explain that this is with the fuel tanks attached.

2. Stretch out the Apollo string again to compare it to that of the shuttle. Be sure the students understand that the Saturn rockets which carried Apollo into space had to be more powerful than the engines used by the shuttle since they had to send them to the moon. Also, the rockets were attached beneath the Apollo command and space modules, thus it appears longer than the shuttle with its fuel tanks attached alongside it.

3. Finally, explain that the space shuttle is not capable of going beyond Earth's orbit as the Apollo spacecraft did.

Space Shuttle

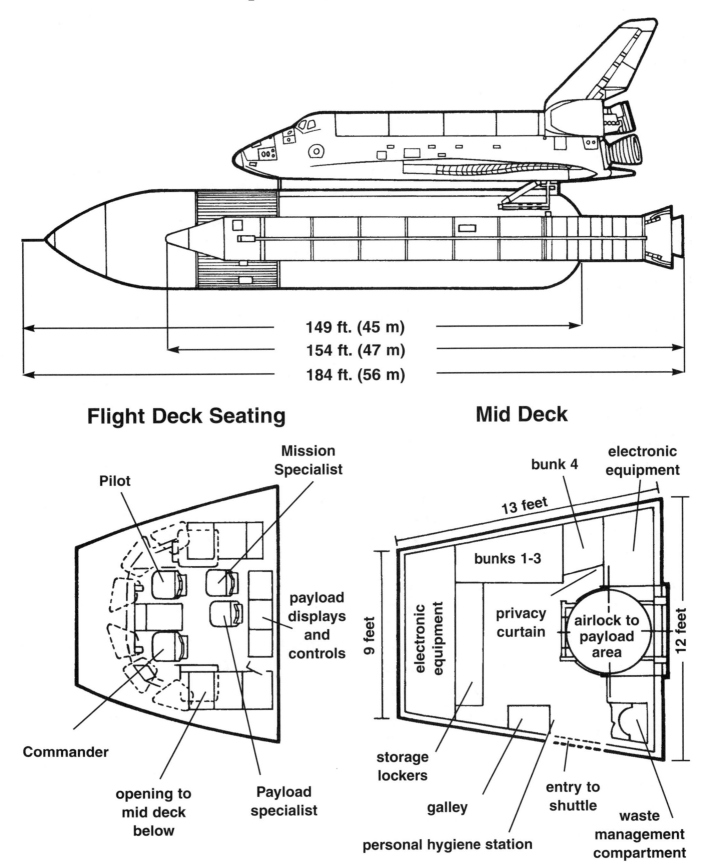

149 ft. (45 m)
154 ft. (47 m)
184 ft. (56 m)

Flight Deck Seating

Pilot

Mission Specialist

payload displays and controls

Commander

opening to mid deck below

Payload specialist

Mid Deck

bunk 4

electronic equipment

13 feet

bunks 1-3

electronic equipment

privacy curtain

airlock to payload area

9 feet

12 feet

storage lockers

galley

personal hygiene station

entry to shuttle

waste management compartment

International Space Station

Teacher Information: Almost the size of two football fields, the International Space Station (ISS) is the largest international space venture ever undertaken. The United States, Russia, Japan, Canada, Italy, Belgium, the Netherlands, Denmark, Norway, France, Spain, Germany, Sweden, Switzerland, the United Kingdom, and Brazil are working on the space station. The ISS will be five times the mass of Skylab. Hauling the parts and pieces of the space station into orbit will require 45 space flights on three different types of launch vehicles over a five-year period. These launches will use the US space shuttle and Russian Proton and Soyuz rockets. The first two sections were launched in late 1998. Once in orbit, these sections, weighing tens of thousands of pounds on Earth but weightless in space, were maneuvered into place by the astronauts. This will continue until all sections are in place. The final connections of cables, switches, wires, tubes, pipes, and fittings will be done by space-suited astronauts.

The central girder connecting the modules and the main solar power arrays will be built by the United States. The Canadians will build a remote manipulator system, a 55-foot (17 m) robot arm, and a grappling mechanism. It will move along the integrated truss (long support arm) on a mobile transporter to perform assembly and maintenance work. The four solar arrays will rotate on the truss to maximize their exposure to the sun.

The pressurized living and working space aboard the completed station will be the size of two passenger cabins of a 747 jetliner. The atmospheric pressure in the station will be 14.7 pounds per square inch, the same as at sea level on Earth. Just as in Skylab or Mir, the crew of six who live on board will wear regular clothes and will float around since there will be only microgravity in the space station.

There will be six laboratories. The US will provide one lab and a habitation module that will replace and supplement the service module's early crew living quarters. There will be two Russian research modules, a Japanese laboratory, and a European Space Agency (ESA) laboratory called the Columbus Orbital Facility (COF).

An emergency crew return vehicle, initially a Russian Soyuz spacecraft and later a higher-capacity vehicle to be developed by NASA, will always be docked with the station while it is inhabited. In addition, a number of vehicles, both with and without people aboard, will be constantly visiting the space station.

Materials: transparency of International Space Station and drawing paper

Procedure:

1. Show the students the transparency of the ISS and explain its components, using the information above. Compare its length with that of Skylab and the space shuttle.

2. Discuss what it would be like to be among the scientists who will work at this space station.

3. Divide the students into small groups and provide each group with drawing paper. Have each group write a story about what it would be like to be part of the crew aboard the ISS and make a drawing to illustrate this story.

Closure:

Have the students share their pictures and read their stories.

International Space Station *(cont.)*

(1)—Functional Cargo Block

(2)—Node 1

(3)—Service Module

(4)—Soyuz Crew Transfer Vehicle

(5)—Universal Docking Module

(6)—Z1

(7)—Solar Power Module and Array

(8)—Science Power Platform

(9)—U.S. Laboratory Module

(10)—Space Station Remote Manipulator System

(11)—Airlock and High Pressure Gas Tanks

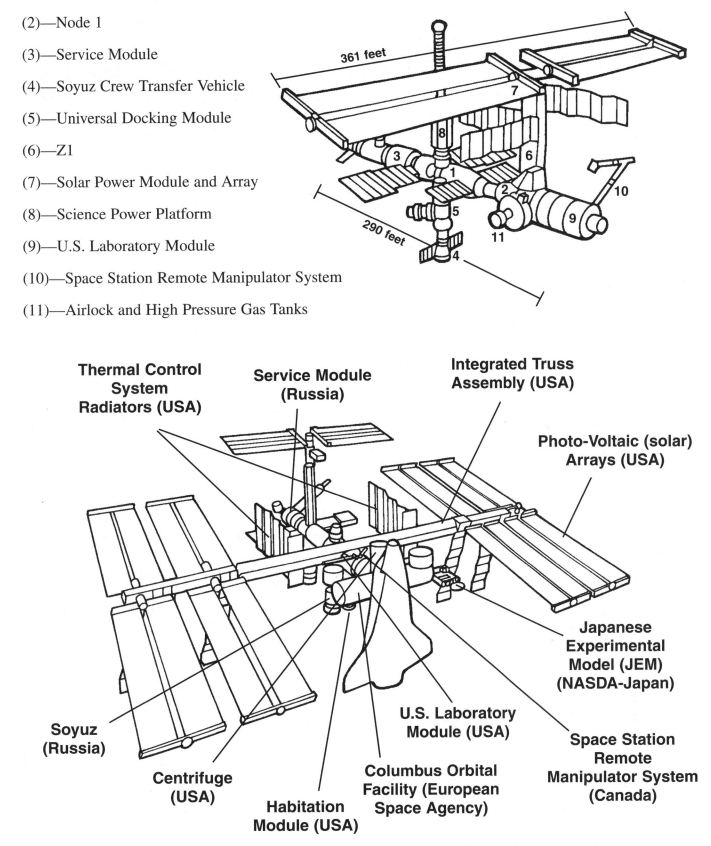

Touring the Solar System

Summary

This final chapter applies much of the learning from the first two chapters as the students become familiar with our solar system. It begins by investigating the origin of planet names and has as its grand finale a play—*Tour of the Solar System*. This play applies much of what the students have studied and serves as the culminating activity for this thematic unit.

Overview of Activities

This chapter uses a variety of multidisciplinary activities to develop the students' conceptual understanding of our solar system. They are introduced to the sun and its nine planets through a series of activities, including making a sundial, constructing a scale model of the planets, and determining students' weights. A scale model of the solar system is created, and the planets' rotation speeds are calculated. A simulated comet is made, and meteor impact craters are recreated with flour and marbles. Using balloons and straws, rocket propulsion is explored, and then students build their own rocket models, using junk brought from home. The music of *The Planets Suite* by Gustav Holst introduces another perspective of the planets. Finally, students add information they gleaned about the sun, planets and their moons, asteroids, and comets to the script for the play *Tour of the Solar System*.

Supplemental Books

Three books make excellent supplements for the lessons in this chapter. Two of these were used in the first chapter, and the third is a humorous and scientifically accurate tour of the solar system aboard *The Magic School Bus*®.

Exploring the Night Sky (See the description on page 6.) Use the chapter Alien Vistas (pages 26–40) to provide information for students' research on the planets and the sun. The chapter "A Cosmic Voyage" (pages 7–25) is an imaginary voyage from Earth to 300,000 light years distance from Earth at the speed of light. This is an excellent way for students to realize how tiny our solar system is. It can be read aloud at the end of this unit.

The Night Sky (See the description on page 6.) Use chapter eight for information and activities about meteors.

The Magic School Bus® *Lost in the Solar System* by Joanna Cole. Ms. Frizzle's class is off for a tour aboard the magic bus to explore the sun, planets, and asteroid belt. Excitement occurs when The Friz leaves the bus to repair damage while in the asteroid belt and is left behind by the bus. The students continue the trip, using their teacher's notes to learn about the planets. They manage to get Ms. Frizzle back on board before returning to Earth.

If possible, get copies for the students to read this delightful book in small groups and use as one of their references as they gather information for their solar system play script.

Extending This Chapter

Subscribe to *Sky Calendar* (see Resources), a monthly calendar which provides detailed information of astronomical views and events. Use this to expand the study of astronomy and to develop student enjoyment of stargazing.

Planets of the Gods

The names of the sun and the planets in the solar system come from Greek and Roman gods which were very important in these ancient civilizations. Complete this booklet, showing the symbol for each planet and give information about the name and symbol. The information for the sun has been done as an example.

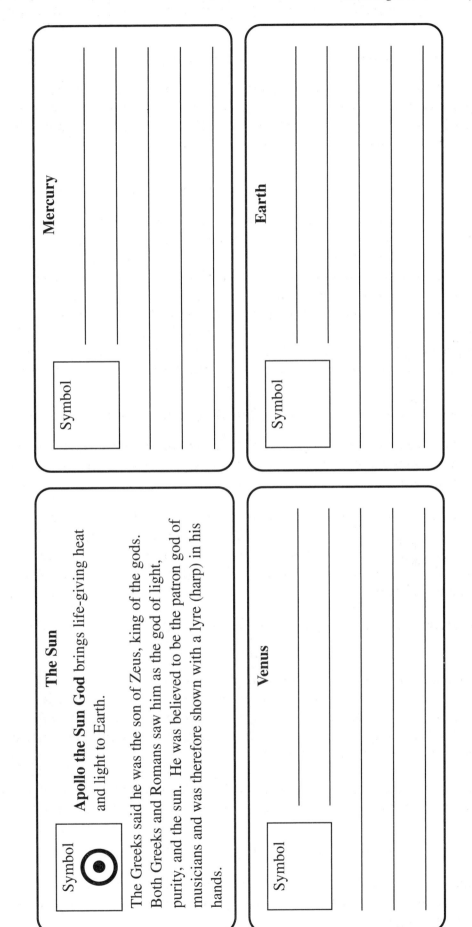

The Sun

Symbol

Apollo the Sun God brings life-giving heat and light to Earth.

The Greeks said he was the son of Zeus, king of the gods. Both Greeks and Romans saw him as the god of light, purity, and the sun. He was believed to be the patron god of musicians and was therefore shown with a lyre (harp) in his hands.

Mercury

Symbol

Venus

Symbol

Earth

Symbol

Planets of the Gods *(cont.)*

Jupiter

Symbol

Uranus

Symbol

Pluto

Symbol

Mars

Symbol

Saturn

Symbol

Neptune

Symbol

How to Make a Sundial

Teacher Information: Using a moving shadow to measure time is a natural extension of the lesson Following the Sun (page 10). No one knows when sundials were designed to tell time. It is believed that the Babylonians used them as early as 2000 B.C. Sundials use the shadow falling across a dial face which has lines at different angles to indicate the hours. The hour angles on the sundial depend upon the latitude. The shadow maker *(gnomon)* may be a piece of metal or wire forming an angle with the sundial plate that is equal to the latitude. It must point to geographic (not magnetic) north to align with Earth's axis pointing to the North Star. Due to the 23½-degrees tilt of Earth's axis and the variation in speed with which it orbits the sun, a sundial agrees with the clock only on April 16, June 14, September 2, and December 25.

Materials for each student: protractor, copy of the sundial template on page 55, 6-inch (15 cm) string (which will cast a shadow and thus serve as the gnomon)

Materials for the teacher: toothpick, globe, transparencies of sundial template and a protractor, completed sundial, shadow record from Following the Sun (page 10)

Lesson Preparation:

Make a sundial to use as a model for the students. On the board copy the sundial angles from the chart below to find the latitude nearest to you.

Sundial Angles for Northern Latitudes 20–55
(rounded to nearest degree)

Latitude	7 A.M.	8 A.M.	9 A.M.	10 A.M.	11 A.M.	1 P.M.	2 P.M.	3 P.M.	4 P.M.	5 P.M.
20°	38°	59°	71°	79°	85°	95°	101°	109°	121°	142°
25°	32°	54°	67°	76°	83°	97°	104°	113°	126°	148°
30°	28°	49°	63°	74°	82°	98°	106°	117°	131°	152°
35°	25°	45°	60°	72°	81°	99°	108°	120°	135°	155°
40°	24°	42°	57°	70°	80°	100°	110°	123°	138°	155°
45°	21°	39°	55°	68°	79°	101°	112°	125°	141°	160°
50°	19°	37°	52°	66°	78°	102°	114°	128°	143°	161°
55°	18°	35°	50°	65°	78°	102°	115°	130°	145°	162°

Setting the Stage:

Place the toothpick on the globe location in which you live. This represents the stick which was used in the lesson Following the Sun. Place the globe in the sun and have the students stand where they can observe its shadow. Rotate the globe (Earth) west to east (counterclockwise). Show how the toothpick's shadow moves in the opposite direction of the spinning "Earth." Rotate the Earth again to demonstrate the changing length of the shadow as the sun passes overhead.

Repeat the demonstration and compare it to the shadow record made in the previous lesson. Tell students that long before there were clocks, people discovered they could use a shadow to help them tell time during the day. This led to the development of the sundial. Tell the students they will each make a sundial to tell time by the sun.

How to Make a Sundial *(cont.)*

Procedure:

1. Distribute the materials to each student.

2. Use the transparency of the sundial template and a protractor to demonstrate how to place the bottom line of the protractor on top of the 6 A.M.–6 P.M. line. The 90° of the protractor should be superimposed on the noon line.

3. Show how to mark the angle for 7 A.M. and have students do this on their sundials. Make sure they do this correctly before proceeding. (Lines for angles will be drawn in once all marks have been made.)

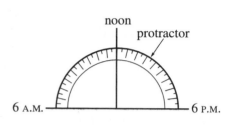

4. Without moving the protractor, have a volunteer draw the mark for 8 A.M. Then have all students do this on their sundials.

5. Let students continue drawing marks to indicate the hour angles from 9 A.M. through 5 P.M., using the data for your latitude.

6. When all marks have been drawn, show the students how to connect the mark to the intersection of the base line (6 A.M./P.M.) and the noon line. They should use sharp pencils to make sure the lines all meet at the same point.

7. Have students cut a slit at the bottom of the sundial as indicated. The slit should stop at the base line. Place the string in the slit with about 1 inch (2.5 cm) behind the sundial. Tape this piece securely behind the sundial.

8. Fold the sundial along the line indicated to form a 90° angle. Cut a shallow slit at the top of the sundial, pull the rest of the string through it, and then measure the angle at the base with the protractor. Adjust the length of the slit until this angle equals your latitude angle. Tape this string to the back of the sundial.

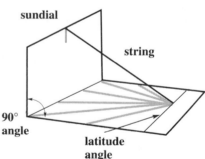

Closure:

- Test sundials by placing them on a flat paved area in the sun.

- Have students adjust their sundials until the shadow cast by the string (gnomon) falls on the hour angle showing the current time.

- Place a small weight on each sundial to hold it in place and then have the students look at all the sundials to discover which way they are all pointing (in the same direction, approximately north). Explain that for a sundial to work properly, the string (gnomon) must point to true north to line up with Earth's axis.

- Have students use chalk to draw around the bases of their sundials and then remove the bases and write their names inside the outlines. Return to the same spot later and recheck the sundials.

- Let students create their own sundials, using various materials for the dial and gnomon. The angles need to remain the same as those used on this sundial.

54

Sundial Template

Cut a slit along the middle of this top line so the gnomon string will form an angle with the base of the sundial equal to your latitude.

Sundial for _____° North Latitude

Designed by:

Fold along this line to form a 90° angle.

Cut all the way around the dark outline of the sundial.

12 P.M. | **noon**

6 A.M.

6 P.M.

Cut a slit here for the gnomon string. ➡

Scale Model of the Planets

Teacher Directions: Have students complete the Planet Cards (pages 58 and 59). Provide them with resources to find more interesting facts about the planets. (See the Resources section.) The following information can be used to create enlarged versions of the planets shown on the Planet Cards. These larger planet models will enable students to understand the vast differences among the giant planets and the smaller planets. The teacher may wish to make these models, or if the students are capable, they may work in small groups to make them.

Materials: five small pieces of colored construction paper, four large pieces of butcher paper, pencil compass, meter stick, metric ruler, overhead projector, 11 meters of string, Planet Cards, file cards

Lesson Preparation:

1. Use a scale so that Earth's diameter of 7,973 miles (12,756 km) is equal to 10 cm. Draw circles for the smaller planets on colored construction paper, using the radius indicated in the chart.

Planet	Model Radius	Color
Mercury	1.9 cm	gray
Venus	4.8 cm	white
Earth	5 cm	blue
Mars	2.7 cm	red
Pluto	0.9 cm	black

2. Make enlarged copies of the four largest planets shown below and then copy them onto a transparency. Project them individually onto large pieces of butcher paper. The radius should be equal to that shown on the chart below. Draw only semicircles for Jupiter and Saturn. Do not include the rings in this model.

Planet	Model Radius	Color
Jupiter	56 cm	red
Saturn	47 cm	yellow
Uranus	20 cm	green
Neptune	19.5 cm	blue

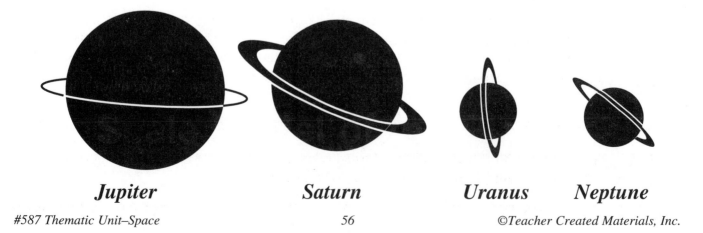

| *Jupiter* | *Saturn* | *Uranus* | *Neptune* |

Scale Model of the Planets *(cont.)*

Procedure:

1. Place these planets on a bulletin board so they are superimposed as shown below.

Sun's Diameter (10.9 meters on this scale)

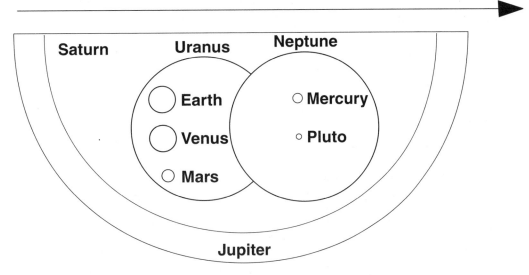

2. Have the students use the Earth model to compare to the diameter of Jupiter as follows:

    *   Tell them to write a guess for the number of Earths they think will fit across Jupiter.
    *   Fold the Earth model in half and use it to measure, beginning at one edge of Jupiter's diameter. Stop after going part way and ask students to update their guesses (they now become predictions).
    *   Continue until you have measured nearly ³/₄ of the diameter. Have students update their predictions. Continue measuring until students discover that about 11 Earths will fit.

3. Use the models to compare the diameter of Earth to the other planets.

Closure:

1. Make a model of the sun's diameter, using string. (It is much too large to do on paper.) The sun is 864,000 miles in diameter. This string, measured to the same scale as that used for the planets, will need to be 10.9 meters long.

2. Tape the planets together, using Jupiter as the base as shown in the drawing.

3. Take the students outside and have two students hold the planets. Tell them you are going to show them how large the sun is on this model, using the same scale. Hand the end of the sun string to the person holding the left edge of Jupiter and stretch the string across the planets and out to its full length. Students will realize that the sun is much larger than all the planets put together.

4. Explain that the sun is a star, not a planet. Tell them that as star sizes go, the sun is average sized. Some stars are much larger; these are giant, red stars. Betelgeuse, a red star in the constellation Orion, is 433 million miles in diameter. It is so huge that if it were in the center of our solar system, Mercury, Venus, Earth, and Mars would be inside it.

Planet Cards

To the Student: The planets shown on these cards are drawn to scale so you can compare their sizes. The numbers show their order from the sun. Use the Planetary Facts chart on page 61 to write the diameter of the planet and its distance from the sun. Look up interesting facts for each planet, using the Planetary Facts and at least three other resources.

1 **Mercury** •	2 **Venus** ●
Diameter = _____	Diameter = _____
Distance from the sun =_____	Distance from the sun =_____
Fascinating Facts:_____	Fascinating Facts:_____
_____	_____
_____	_____
3 **Earth** ●	4 **Mars** •
Diameter = _____	Diameter = _____
Distance from the sun =_____	Distance from the sun =_____
Fascinating Facts:_____	Fascinating Facts:_____
_____	_____
_____	_____
5 **Jupiter**	6 **Saturn**
Diameter = _____	Diameter = _____
Distance from the sun =	Distance from the sun =
_____	_____
Fascinating Facts:_____	Fascinating Facts:_____
_____	_____

Planet Cards *(cont.)*

To the Student: Finish writing the diameter, distance, and new information on these last three planet cards. Answer the questions about each of the cards. Cut out all the cards and then glue them to individual file cards. Add new information about the planets which you learn as you continue doing the lessons in this book.

7	**Uranus**

Diameter =
_____

Distance from
the sun =
_____

Fascinating Facts:_____

_____

_____

8	**Neptune**

Diameter =
_____

Distance from
the sun =
_____

Fascinating Facts:_____

_____

_____

9	**Pluto**	•

Diameter = _____

Distance from the sun =_____

Fascinating Facts:_____

_____

_____

List the planets in order from the sun:

1._____
2._____
3._____
4._____
5._____
6._____
7._____
8._____
9._____

List the planets in order of their size:

1._____
2._____
3._____
4._____
5._____
6._____
7._____
8._____
9._____

On the size list of the planets, circle those which have rings. Write what you have just discovered about these planets.

_____

_____

Look at the sizes of the four planets which are closest to the sun. Compare their sizes to the next four planets. Write what you have discovered.

_____

_____

Scale Model of the Solar System

Teacher Directions: Have students use the Planetary Facts on page 61 to create a scale model of the solar system. Planet distances from the sun will be represented by strings. Earth's distance from the sun (1 AU) will be reduced to one meter (3 feet) for this model. (Students should use metric measurements.)

Materials: 91 meters (300 feet) of string, nine meter (29.5 feet) sticks, nine pieces of heavy cardboard 13 cm x 20 cm (5" x 8") nine metal washers, nine copies of the Planetary Facts chart

Procedure:

1. Divide students into nine groups and distribute a meter stick, cardboard, metal washer, and copy of Planetary Facts to each group. Explain the model construction and the scale.

2. Assign a different planet to each group and have them circle the Astronomical Units (AU) for their planet on their chart. Tell them they will need a string equal to the length of the AU multiplied by one meter. Have them write the length of their string on the chart above the AU for their planet. Check each group's calculations before they cut the string.

    (Examples: Venus = .7 AU x 1 meter = .7 meter; Pluto = 39.7 AU x 1 meter = 39.7 meters)

3. Label the cardboard with the planet's name and distance from the sun. Attach the string to the cardboard, wind it around the cardboard, and attach the metal washer to its end to keep it from fraying. Be sure students are exact in their measurements. (**Note:** Groups doing planets beyond Jupiter will need more string and time for their part of this model.)

Closure:

1. Stretch out the solar system model to show the inner planets from the sun to Mars. Let a volunteer represent the sun, holding the washer at the end of the strings for Mercury, Venus, and Earth. The strings should be stretched from the sun in a straight line to compare lengths. Point out how close these planets appear but remind them that Earth is really 93 million miles from the sun. Add Jupiter so the students will see the vast distance between this planet and Mars. Between Mars and Jupiter is the asteroid belt.

2. Wind up the strings and move outside to reconstruct the entire model. Ask three students to be the sun; each will hold three washers. Have groups unwind their planet strings, one at a time; start with Mercury in straight lines for easy comparison.

3. Have them lay the strings down so all can "walk through the solar system." As they reach Pluto, have them look back. Ask them what the sun would look like from Pluto (a faint star).

4. Explain that planets do not move around the sun in a straight path, but all go counterclockwise around the sun. All planets except Pluto are on the same plane as the sun, like being on a large plate with the sun in the center. Pluto's orbit is tilted and more elliptical than the others. It sometimes comes inside Neptune's orbit, but they are too far apart to ever collide. Pluto was closer to the sun than Neptune from January 1979 to March 1999.

5. The nearest star to our solar system, on this scale, would be 280 km (174 miles) away!

Planetary Facts

Categories	Mercury	Venus	Earth	Mars	Jupiter	Saturn	Uranus	Neptune	Pluto
Diameter in miles: (kilometers)	3,050 (4,880)	7,563 (12,100)	7,973 (12,756)	4,246 (6,794)	89,365 (142,984)	75,335 (120,536)	31,938 (51,100)	30,938 (49,500)	1,438 (2,300)
Diameters relative to Earth's:	.38	.95	1.0	.53	11.2	9.4	4	3.9	.18
Average distance from sun in millions of miles: (kilometers)	36 (57.9)	67 (108.2)	93 (149.6)	142 (227.9)	486 (778.3)	893 (1,429)	1,797 (2,875)	2,815 (4,504)	3,688 (5,900)
Relative to Earth's distance from the sun:	0.4 AU*	0.7 AU*	1.0 AU*	1.5 AU*	5.2 AU*	9.6 AU*	19.3 AU*	30.3 AU*	39.7 AU*
Length of year (trip around the sun):	88 days	224.7 days	365.3 days	687 days	11.86 years	29.46 years	84 years	165 years	248 years
Length of day (turn around once on axis):	59 days	243 days Retro**	23 h. 56 m.	24 h. 37 m.	9 h. 55 m.	10 h. 40 m.	17 h. 18 m. Retro**	16 h. 7 m.	6 days 9 h. 18 m. Retro**
Gravity at surface:	.38 g	.91 g	1.0 g	.38 g	2.53 g	1.07 g	.91 g	1.16 g	.05 g (?)
Number of moons:	0	0	1	2	16	18	15	8	1
Number of rings:	0	0	0	0	3	1,000 (?)	11	4	0

*AU=Astronomical Unit, average distance between Earth and sun is 93 million miles (149.6 million kilometers). The data below each planet shows its distance in astronomical units.

**Retro=retrograde or backwards motion from the rest of the planets. Earth turns (rotates) on its axis from west to east; planets which have retrograde motion rotate east to west.

These statistics were taken from the most recent information available from NASA and other reliable sources. You may find different data in more recent articles since this information is continuously being revised through the use of new equipment.

How Fast Are Planets Moving?

Because the planet we live on seems so stable, it is sometimes hard to believe that we are always moving. So just how fast is Earth moving? To find this out you will need to find the circumference (distance around a circle) of Earth's equator. Do the following activity to discover how to find the circumference of a planet by just knowing its diameter. With this information you will then be able to figure the speed of the planet.

Directions:

You will need a metric measuring tape, tape, blank paper, pencil compass, and a calculator. Use the compass to draw three circles with the diameters of 5, 8, and 12 cm. Write the sizes of the diameters on the circles. Cut out the circles and tape them to a table to measure them. Stand the tape measure on its edge and wrap it carefully around the circle to find its circumference. Repeat this several times to be sure you are accurate and then record the circumference. Now, make a circle with a different diameter of your choice and measure its circumference.

Use a calculator to discover the relationship between the diameter and the circumference.

Circumference (measured to nearest cm)	÷ Diameter	= Results
Circle 1 _____	5 cm	
Circle 2 _____	8 cm	
Circle 3 _____	12 cm	
Circle 4 _____ (your choice)	_____ cm	

Did you notice that the results are always about 3.14? Long ago, mathematicians discovered that no matter what the size of the circle, the circumference was always 3.14 times as large as the diameter. This number is referred to by the Greek letter π (pi), and it can be used to find the circumference of Earth and other planets.

Diameter of Earth _____ mi. (_____ km) x 3.14 = _____ mi.
(_____ km) circumference at the equator

To find the speed of the earth at the equator, complete the following:

Circumference _____ ÷ _____ number of hours in a day = _____ mi.
(_____ km) per hour

How Fast Are Planets Moving? *(cont.)*

Using what you learned on the previous page and the information below, calculate the approximate speeds of the nine planets in our solar system. Follow the steps below.

	Mercury	Venus	Earth	Mars	Jupiter	Saturn	Uranus	Neptune	Pluto
Diameter in Miles	3,050	7,563	7,973	4,246	89,365	75,335	31,938	30,938	1,438
Hours in a Day	1,416	5,832	24	25	10	11	17	16	153

(**Note:** The hours for each planet have been rounded and are not exact.)

1. Use your calculator to find the circumference of each planet by multiplying each diameter by 3.14.

2. Write each planet's circumference in the chart below.

3. Use your calculator to divide each circumference by the number of hours in the day of each planet. The answer to this calculation will give you the speed at which the planet moves.

	Circumference	÷ Hours in a Day	= Miles Per Hour
Mercury			
Venus			
Earth			
Mars			
Jupiter			
Saturn			
Uranus			
Neptune			
Pluto			

Comets

Teacher Directions: Before doing the demonstration below, discuss with your students the general information in the box.

> Astronomer Dr. Fred Whipple called comets "dirty snowballs" because of their appearance. In fact, the nucleus, or core, of a comet does resemble a large snowball. The core can be from $^1/_2$ to 32 miles (1–51 km) in diameter and is made of small particles of gravel or large boulders embedded in frozen gases. When a comet travels close to the sun, the ice turns into a gas. The sun's radiation makes the gas glow, creating the *coma* around the core. Some gas and particles are forced away from the comet, creating a tail which is longest when the comet is near the sun.
>
> The astronomer Edmund Halley realized that comets travel in orbits. He recognized a comet he had observed as being the same one that had been seen and written about 75 years before and even 75 years before that. This comet, now known as Halley's Comet, is still in an orbit which comes near Earth every 75 years. There are hundreds of recorded comets, some of them with orbit periods millions of years long!

Demonstration—What Does a Comet Look Like?

Materials: large plastic bag, 2 cups (480 mL) water, ammonia, 2 spoonfuls of sand, 10 pounds (4.5 kg) of dry ice, large bowl or tray, hammer, gloves, large wooden or metal spoon

(**Note:** To purchase dry ice, check the telephone directory or ice-cream shops. It is extremely cold and should be handled with gloves. It evaporates rapidly and should be used soon after purchase. If it is to be stored for a few hours, wrap it in layers of paper and store it in an ice chest, not a freezer.)

Procedure:

Use the hammer to break the dry ice into golf ball-sized pieces. Put the pieces into the plastic bag; they represent the largest ingredient of the comet, the frozen gas of carbon dioxide. Pour the water, a few drops of ammonia, and sand into the bag and mix these with the dry ice to form a large ball. After the ball is as tightly packed as possible, dump it into the bowl. At this point carbon dioxide gas will be given off as the dry ice begins to warm and evaporate. The gas is heavier than atmospheric gases and thus begins to roll down toward the floor. This gas is harmless in a room where fresh air is free to enter and provide oxygen to breathe.

Now, try blowing on your comet to simulate the heat of the sun and watch the tail rush away from you. Give your comet a name and place it where it can be observed as it evaporates.

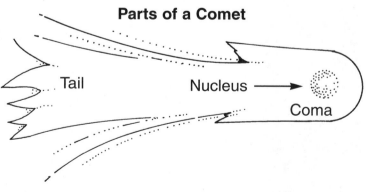

Parts of a Comet

Tail   Nucleus
                       Coma

The gas escaping from the nucleus of the comet creates the coma and tail, which only become visible as a comet passes near the sun and heats up. The tail may be 600,000 to 60 million miles (965,606 to 96 million km) long. It is always pushed away from the comet by the sun's radiation, even when the comet is moving away from the sun. Listen to the sounds your comet makes. It should pop and whistle as it evaporates, just as a real comet would. Jets of gas escaping make the comet tumble as it travels in its orbit.

Meteors

Teacher Directions: Before doing the demonstration below, read to or discuss with your students the general meteor information in the box.

When people of ancient times saw a streak of light moving across the sky, they thought a star was falling. While we still use the terms *falling star* and *shooting star* to describe these streaks, scientists today realize that these are actually meteors. Meteors are made up of stone and/or metallic pieces. As a comet travels, it loses pieces of its nucleus as it melts, leaving them in its path across the orbits of the planets. When Earth passes through these areas of comet dust in its orbit, gravity pulls some of it into our atmosphere. Friction from the air burns up the dust, leaving a bright flash and sometimes even a streak if the chunk is large. These are called meteors. Meteor showers can be predicted since Earth revisits these same areas of deposits in its orbit every year.

Meteors have three possible stages. When they are far out in space and not yet in Earth's atmosphere, they are called *meteoroids*. If they enter into Earth's atmosphere, they are then called *meteors*. And, the few meteors which survive the journey and actually reach the earth's surface are called *meteorites*. If a meteorite strikes our planet, its impact may cause a large hole in the ground. This hole is known as a *crater.*

Demonstration—How Are Craters Created?

Materials: flour, a rectangular cake pan, small pebbles, and newspaper

Procedure:

1. Fill the cake pan to the top with flour. Save some flour separately to use in step three. Smooth the pan's flour surface by pulling some sort of straight-edged item (such as a ruler) over the top.

2. Spread several sheets of newspaper on the floor of the demonstration area. Place the pan in the center of the newspaper.

3. Stand on a chair above the pan of flour. Drop a pebble into the pan. Repeat this procedure from different heights and with different-sized pebbles and notice the differences.

The pan represents the surface of Earth or the moon. The pebbles represent the meteorites which reach the surface. As the pebbles impact the flour surface, they should create crater-like formations, including the sloped sides and rims. Changing the height from which the pebbles are dropped and the sizes of the pebbles should change the size and depth of the flour craters. This is similar to real meteorites in that their size and speed affect the size and depth of the craters they make.

Rocket Science

Teacher Directions: Space rockets need to use a great deal of force to be propelled into outer space. What is it that causes the forward motion of a rocket? The following physical science activity will illustrate for your students Sir Isaac Newton's theory that "for every action there is an equal and opposite reaction." In this case the "action" of the gases escaping the balloon will cause the "reaction" of the rocket moving forward.

Materials:

- 1 hot dog-shaped balloon (total number of balloons depends on whether your students will be doing this in groups or as individuals)
- 1 piece of string at least 10 feet (3 meters) long
- 1 drinking straw
- masking tape
- yardsticks or measuring tapes
- a copy of the data capture sheet and diagrams for each group (page 67)

Procedure:

1. Feed the string through the straw.

2. Determine a flight pattern for the rocket. There are a variety of options, all of which can be employed for comparative purposes. Here are some suggestions:

   - Two students hold the ends of the string in a level fashion.
   - Attach one end of the string to the wall with tape or a pushpin. (Be sure the string is level with the student.)
   - Attach one end of the string to the ceiling.
   - Attach each end of the string to the back of a chair. (This option has been illustrated for you on page 67.)

3. Attach three pieces of tape to the straw. Inflate the balloon, but just pinch it off instead of tying it. While pinching the balloon, attach it to the straw and tape. (See the diagram on page 67.)

4. Make predictions about the distance the balloon will travel. Discuss whether the direction (up or across) will make any variation. Record predictions.

5. At the starting signal, instruct the students to release the balloons and watch them fly across (or up) the strings. (See the diagram on page 67.)

You may wish to extend this activity by having your students add additional balloons (increased thrust) and weight (increased load) to the experiment and observe the results. Also, try balloons of different shapes and sizes and observe and record any variations in speed and distance.

Finally, ask your students to summarize the phenomenon of force that was used in this experiment. Students should complete the data capture sheet in order to help them reconstruct and explain the experiment. Through group discussions, encourage your students to come up with some universal principles that were used.

Rocket Science *(cont.)*

Data Capture Sheet

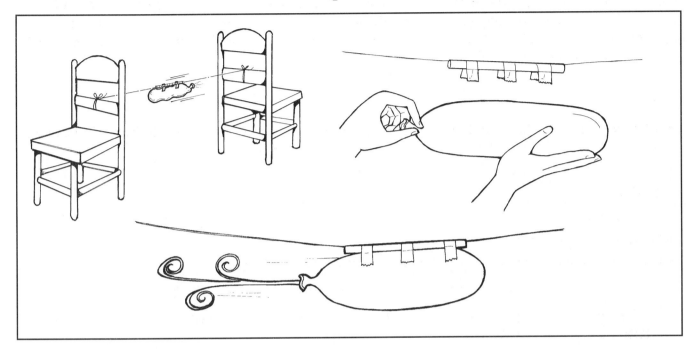

Initial Estimate: With your partner or group, make an estimate of the distance the rocket balloon will fly before coming to a stop. (Be sure to include the unit of measurement.)

Our measurement estimate is_____.

Actual Measurement: Measure the distance the rocket balloon flew from starting to stopping point.

The actual measurement was_____.

Difference: If there is a difference, do the necessary calculation and record the answer.

The difference between our estimate and the actual measurement is_____.

Now try creating a different flight pattern. Follow the above format for the next set of rocket trials. Be sure to note any changes of variables that you might add, such as using the ceiling, a wall, two people, etc.

Estimate	Flight Pattern	Actual	Difference

Building a Future Space Vehicle

Teacher Information: The students will create rockets from a variety of "junk" such as Styrofoam packing blocks, aluminum foil, wire, and cardboard tubes. They should be as creative as possible in this endeavor, using pictures of past, present, and future space vehicles to inspire them.

Materials: a variety of materials students bring from home, glue gun, gold and silver spray paint, pictures of past, present, and future space vehicles

Lesson Preparation:

Compose a letter to the parents to let them know about the present study of space in which their children are involved. Explain that you have assigned them to work in small groups to construct a future space vehicle from a variety of materials they will bring from home. Make a partial list of items to include in the letter as examples.

Procedure:

1. Show the students pictures of the space vehicles. Tell them that they are going to work in small groups to construct a space vehicle which will be capable of touring the solar system.

2. Let them know that it is their responsibility to bring the materials from home that they will need for their space vehicle.

3. When the materials have been gathered, divide the students into groups of three or four. Have each group consider what materials they have and how best to use them as they build their future space vehicle. Allow sufficient time for trial and error as they work.

4. Offer assistance in some tasks which require using the glue gun or spray paint. Be sure spray painting is done outside where the fumes will not build up to create breathing problems.

Closure:

When the space vehicles are completed, have each group write a brief description to accompany their model and put them on display.

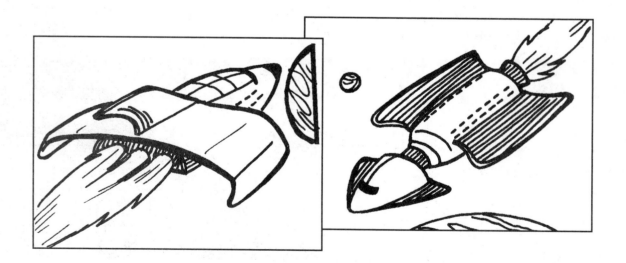

Cosmic Music

Listen to the Planets

Gustav Holst (1874–1934) was an English composer and teacher. One of his most famous pieces of music was the suite *The Planets*. This consisted of seven planets: Mercury, Venus, Mars, Jupiter, Saturn, Uranus, and Neptune. The music was based upon the astrological nature of each planet. This activity asks the students to listen to some of this suite and draw what they imagine as the music is playing.

1. Display the photographs of the seven planets used in the suite of music *The Planets*. Include pictures of the four Galilean moons of Jupiter. (See NASA and the book *Our Universe* in the Resources section.)

2. Tell the background of *The Planets* suite to the students.

3. Ask the students why Holst did not include Earth or Pluto in his music. (*Earth was not included since it is not seen in the zodiac. Pluto had not been discovered when this was composed.*)

4. Review some of the things they have learned about the planets and additional information given with the NASA photographs.

5. Tell the students that you are going to play the Jupiter section of the suite and that you want them to listen to it with their eyes closed so they can concentrate on it.

6. Remind them that Jupiter has $2\frac{1}{2}$ times the gravity of Earth, spins nearly 28 times faster, and has intense pressure in the rapidly swirling gases of its atmosphere. Ask them to think of what it would be like to be inside the giant storm of the red spot on Jupiter. Tell them to imagine creatures which might live under these conditions.

7. Show the pictures and tell about the Galilean moons near Jupiter (Io, Europa, Ganymede, and Callisto).

8. After playing the Jupiter section, distribute white paper to the students and have them listen to it again. This time, have them make drawings of what they are imagining as they hear the music.

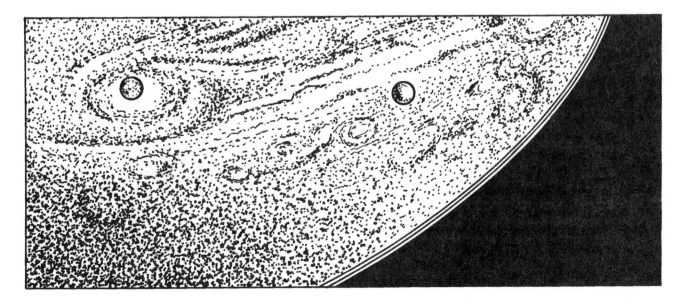

Space Play: *Tour of the Solar System*

Teacher Instructions: The play used in this lesson will apply what the students have learned about the solar system. It is designed to be performed on stage to permit sufficient space and lighting as written. If performed elsewhere, make the necessary adjustments to fit the facilities being used.

Materials: copies of *The Magic School Bus Lost in the Solar System*®, *Tour of the Solar System* script, large cardboard for scenery panels, butcher paper, pictures for script, two overhead projectors, two tables, chairs, yarn, glass bottle, newspaper, hammer, tennis ball, aluminum foil, coffee can and pebbles, transparency pen, dark blue plastic theme covers or cellophane sheets, sheet of black construction paper

Lesson Preparation:

1. Purchase a copy of *The Magic School Bus Lost in the Solar System.*® (See Resources section.) If possible, get enough copies so students can read them aloud in small groups.
2. Wrap the glass bottle in layers of newspapers so it can be broken during the play with the hammer and no glass will fly out. Put aluminum foil around the tennis ball to make it lumpy. It is the asteroid for the play. Place the pebbles in the coffee can and put the lid on it.
3. Make a transparency of the solar system map to project on a scenery panel.
4. Gather pictures referred to in the script and make colored transparencies of these photographs. (see Resources). Colored transparencies can be made at most copy service shops.
5. Cut the theme covers into 2 x 9-inch (5 cm x 23 cm) wide strips, punch holes in each end and tie a 6-inch (15 cm) string through each hole. These are used by the cast and passengers in the play for eye protection.
6. Draw the stars for the constellation Leo on black construction paper and punch holes in the stars with a pin. Make a slightly larger hole to represent the sun as seen from Neptune.

Procedure:

1. Read *The Magic School Bus Lost in the Solar System*® aloud to the students or have them read their copies in small groups. Discuss the information they gleaned from this book.
2. Tell the students that they are going to present *Tour of the Solar System,* a play which will take them on an imaginary tour of the solar system similar to that of Ms. Frizzle's class. Explain that you need their help in completing the script with information about what they will see during the tour. Show the following list of 12 topics and then form small groups of students for each topic.

Solar System Tour Topics

Mercury	Mars and moons	Uranus and moons	sun
Venus	Jupiters and moons	Neptune and moons	comets
Earth and moon	Saturn and moons	Pluto and moon	asteroids

3. Have students collect information on their topics and add it to the script.
4. Follow the suggestions for scenery and staging. Have students draw dials, switches, and computer monitors for the control panels. Select cast members and stage hands. If stage lighting is available, use it during the play to add special effects.

Closure:

Present the play to parents, guests, and other classes as the culmination of this thematic unit.

Space Play: *Tour of the Solar System* *(cont.)*

Scenery: Make the scenery panels from large cardboard. Cut a hole for the window and cover it with white paper. Cut another sheet of white paper large enough to cover the window. Tape it above the window on the back of the scenery panel. Roll it up and hold it in place with larger paper clips at each end. This will need to be rolled down near the end of the play as a shield over the window.

Paste the student-made dials, switches, and computer monitors on the control panels. Cover one scenery panel with white paper. Place the overhead projector in front of it as shown in the diagram.

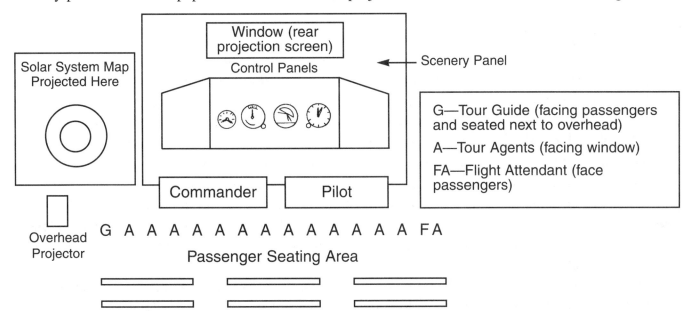

Images: Place one overhead projector behind the scenery so the image will be projected on the white paper and fill the window. This image will appear in reverse to the audience, so turn the transparencies over. The color and pictures will be clearly visible. Put the pictures in order as they are to appear during the play.

Cast Members

    (COM) Commander: responsible for flying the spaceship
    (PL) Pilot: second in command, assists Commander
    (FA) Flight Attendant: oversees safety and comfort of passengers
    (TG) Tour Guide: narrator who coordinates tour and introduces tour agents
    (TA) Tour Agents: member from each of the 12 topic groups, presents their information
    (PA 1) Passenger #1: reluctant traveler
    (PA 2) Passenger #2: helpful traveler
    (PA) Passengers: members of the tour group, at least 10
    (SH) Stagehands: operate projector and handle special effects, at least three needed.

Stage Setting: Have the passengers sit in rows, three across as in a large commercial jet plane. They should have their backs to the audience. Use two pieces of yarn tied to each chair as seatbelts. Place desks and chairs for the commander and pilot near the control panels. Place chairs for the tour guide, agents, and flight attendant in front of the passengers as shown. *Optional:* Provide uniforms for the commander, pilot, and flight attendant. These may be constructed from disposable paint overalls which can be dyed and then decorated to look like uniforms.

Space Play: *Tour of the Solar System* (cont.)

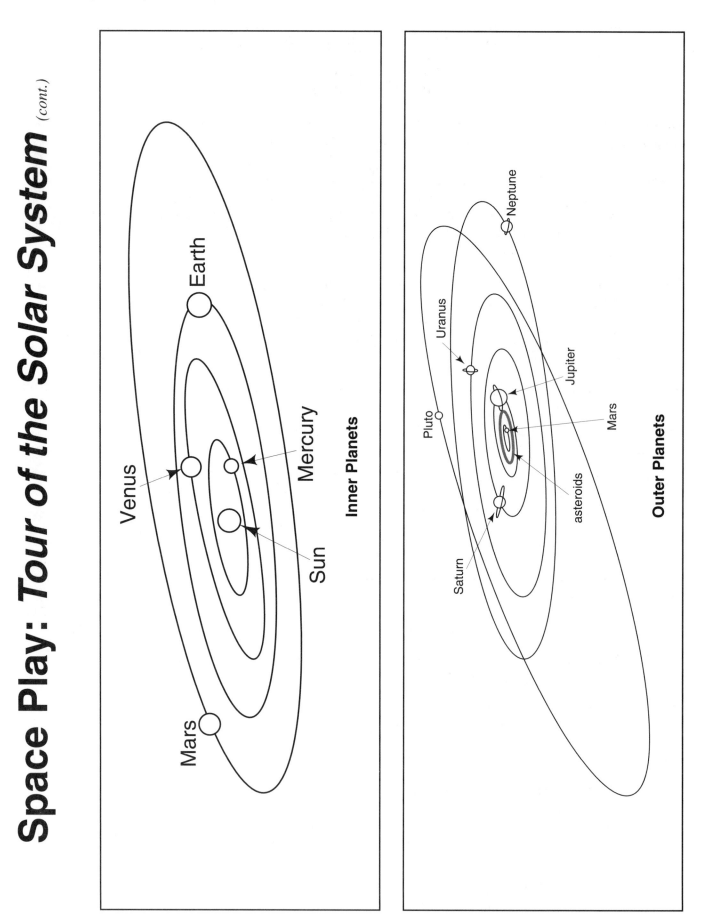

Inner Planets

Earth

Venus

Mercury

Sun

Mars

Outer Planets

Neptune

Uranus

Jupiter

Mars

asteroids

Pluto

Saturn

Space Play: *Tour of the Solar System* *(cont.)*

To the Cast: Directions for the cast members are shown in italics between parentheses. Pictures which coincide with the script are shown in brackets—e.g., [Partial Earth].

COM: This is Commander _____ speaking. On behalf of Pilot _____ and myself, we went to welcome you aboard flight ABC for the grand tour of the solar system. We will be traveling so fast today that our trip will only take about an hour, yet the distance we will travel will be nearly seven billion miles. Please listen to the flight attendant for instructions before takeoff.

FA: While in flight, everyone must stay seated with your seatbelts fastened. Once we blast off from Earth, we will be weightless and would float around. As we take you on this once-in-a-lifetime tour, your tour guide and tour agents will tell you about what we are seeing through this window. Now, just sit back and relax, be sure your seatbelt is fastened securely, and prepare for liftoff.

PL: Ground control, all systems are go. Ready for countdown to begin. Repeating the count from ground control . . . 10 . . . 9 . . . 8 . . . 7 . . . 6 . . . 5 . . . 4 . . . 3 . . . 2 . . . 1 . . . LIFT OFF! We are clearing the launch tower now. Picking up speed 5,000 . . . 8,000 . . . 10,000 miles per hour. Orbital speed of 17,500 mph has been reached, turning engines off.

COM: [Partial Earth] *(To all aboard)* Welcome to outer space, everyone. We are orbiting about 200 miles above Earth. Take a look at that spectacular view. We aren't high enough yet to see the whole planet, but we will as we travel toward the moon.

TG: [Map] *(Show map)* I will use this map of the solar system to show you just where we are throughout the trip. Since the solar system is so large, we are only looking at a map of the inner planets. Right now, we are here *(mark Earth)*. We'll use its gravity to help us get to the moon *(show path)*. The Tour Agent for Earth will tell us about our planet.

TA: *(Tour agent for Earth/moon should describe some of its features.)*

COM: We are preparing to change course to take us to the moon. You will feel the slight thrust of our booster engines, so hold on.

PL: [Full Earth] On course to the moon. Look back at the view of Earth now; we can see all of it. We are about 150,000 miles from home and only 90,000 miles from the moon.

TA: *(Tour agent for Earth/moon should give the rest of the information about Earth.)*

TG: [Distant Earth] *(Mark location on map.)* The moon is not very far from us now. We are closing in fast. There were six landings on the moon by American astronauts from 1969 to 1972—that was over 50 years ago. There is an international colony there now. We won't get to visit there on this trip, however. Let's hear some interesting information about the moon.

TA: [Moon & Future Moon Base] *(Tour agent for Earth/moon tells about the moon.)*

Space Play: *Tour of the Solar System* (cont.)

TG: Take a last look at the moon; we are about to visit another planet—Venus. It is sometimes called Earth's twin, but this is only in size; all else is very different.

PL: Booster rockets firing to set our course for Venus.

TG: [Venus] (*Point to Venus.*) Look at Venus—all we can see are clouds. Tell us about this planet, please. (*Looking at Tour Agent for Venus.*)

TA: (*Tour agent for Venus should tell about this planet.*)

COM: You can see on the solar system map that we are going to need to use the gravity from Venus like a slingshot to push us to Mercury. This is called a gravity assist, and it will save the energy needed by our booster rockets.

TG: [Mercury] (*Draw path part way around Venus and off to Mercury.*) The Mercury tour agent will tell us about this little planet.

TA: (*Tell about the planet Mercury.*)

FA: Since we will be traveling close to the sun, we need to put on special shields to protect our eyes from its intense light. Please tie on the eye shields now. (*All put on shields.*)

PA 1: It sure is getting hot in here! I don't think this trip was such a great idea after all.

PA 2: Don't worry, it will cool down after we pass by the sun. Just think how great it is being so close to the sun. Maybe we'll see sunspots.

TG: [Sun] (*Mark sun on map.*) This is our location now. It is a little warm, so we won't stay long, but this is a spectacular view. Let's hear about the energy sources for all the planets.

TA: (*Describe the features of the sun.*)

COM: Get ready for a real boost in speed; we're going to head out for Mars.

PA 1: I sure don't like it when we speed up like this. I feel like I've just gained a ton.

PA 2: Yes, but think how good it feels when we slow down and become weightless again.

FA: You can remove your eye shields now since we have left the sun behind us. (*Everyone removes eye shields.*)

TG: (*Mark path to Mars on map.*) As you can see on the map, we have to pass through the orbits of Mercury, Venus, and Earth to get to Mars. This planet is one and a half times farther from the sun than Earth but is only half as big as our planet.

TA: [Mars, Martian moons] (*Tour agent for Mars and its moons should tell the information about these.*)

COM: We are entering the asteroid belt now; this can be a dangerous area.

PL: I will try to steer the ship between the asteroids.

COM: Watch out! A swarm of little asteroids are headed our way! Activate protection shield.

SH: (*Rattle pebbles in coffee can.*)

PL: Activating the protection shield now! Just in time, too; that was a close call. Some of those hit us before the shield was up.

Space Play: *Tour of the Solar System* (cont.)

COM: Give me a damage report.

PL: All instruments show we are OK, Commander.

FA: The cabin is secure, and all passengers are OK, Commander.

PA 1: First they tried to fry us, and now we're a target for flying rocks. What next?

PA 2: This is the safest spaceship ever built. I am sure it will make it through.

TG: (*Mark location on map.*) Let's hear about the asteroids. It will calm our nerves.

TA: [Asteroid] (*Tour agent for asteroids tells about these mini-planets.*)

COM: [Martian Colony] We are safely through the asteroid belt and are approaching Mars. A space colony was started here in 2010. It has nearly 5,000 people now. We don't have time to stop on this trip, but you might want to return someday to visit.

TG: [Mars] Our company offers tours to Mars. We are running a special now—two weeks for only a half-million-dollars. If you are interested, I can give you more information. The tour agent for Mars will tell you about this planet, and you will see what a wonderful place it is to visit.

TA: (*Tour agent for Mars gives information about the planet.*)

COM: We are leaving the inner planets as we orbit around Mars, using its gravity to boost us off across the 350-million-mile distance to the largest planet in our solar system.

TG: [Jupiter] (*Mark path to Jupiter on outer planet map.*) This planet is so enormous that 11 Earths could fit across its diameter. At one time people thought only Saturn had rings around it, but when early satellites went past Jupiter, they photographed a faint ring around it.

TA: [Moons of Jupiter] (*Tour agent for Jupiter gives information about the planet.*)

COM: Saturn is on the other side of the sun, so we will go to Neptune next. This is a very long way off, so we will whip around giant Jupiter to use its gravity to push us to Neptune.

FA: Be sure your seatbelts are fastened tightly. This may get to be a bit bumpy. You will feel very heavy as we pass around Jupiter, but don't worry. Once we are out of its gravity grip, you will be weightless again. Here we go—hold on!

PA 1: Oh no! Not another weight gain. I feel like a cement truck!

PA 2: You really wasted your money on this trip. I think it is great!

SH: (*Place the black construction paper on overhead to show Leo. Be sure you see Leo's head on the left so the audience sees it on the right.*)

PL: [Constellation Leo] We have just traveled two billion, three hundred miles. What a ride! Look at the constellation Leo; that extra bright star in it is the sun. We are so far away from the sun now that it looks much smaller and dimmer than it does from Earth.

Space Play: *Tour of the Solar System* (cont.)

TG: [Neptune] (*Mark Neptune's position on map.*) Look how far we have come. You can see that the planets don't orbit the sun in a straight line but are spread out around it. That is why we aren't visiting the planets in order from the sun. Neptune is now the second most distant planet from the sun, but since Pluto's orbit comes inside Neptune's, it is sometimes farther away than Pluto. That happened between January 1979 and March 1999. Since it is now 2022, Neptune is back where it belongs, the eighth planet from the sun. It has rings around it like the other giant planets. Let's hear more about this beautiful blue planet and its moon.

TA: (*Tour agent for Neptune gives information about it.*)

COM: We need to speed up once again, this time to get to Uranus, another giant.

TG: [Uranus] You can see by its rings that it is tipped on its side. Scientists think some huge object like a comet passed so close to Uranus that it was pulled onto its side.

TA: (*Tour agent for Uranus describes the planet.*)

COM: Now, off to the tiniest planet in our solar system, Pluto. We are about three billion miles from the sun. It is totally black out here, and the sun looks like a dim star very far away.

TG: [Pluto, Charon] (*Mark Pluto's location on map.*) This tiny planet is so far from Earth that it wasn't discovered until 1930. It is named for the Roman god of the dark underworld. Listen to some interesting facts about this planet and its tiny moon, Charon.

TA: (*Tour agent for Pluto tells about this planet.*)

COM: Prepare for our ride back across the orbits of Neptune and Uranus to reach Saturn.

PL: [Saturn] We have made the trip safely and in record time. There is Saturn—look at those spectacular rings!

TG: [Saturn's rings] (*Mark Saturn on map.*) Although the other giant planets of Jupiter, Uranus, and Neptune also have rings, Saturn's rings were the first to be seen through a telescope. From close up they look like freeways made by orbiting rock and ice chunks. The tour agent for Saturn will tell you all about this huge planet.

TA: (*Tour agent for Saturn explains what this planet is like.*)

TG: (*Mark location at Saturn and draw path to Earth's orbit.*) We have toured all the nine planets in our solar system and are now preparing for the huge leap back to Earth. Look, there is a special treat for us—a comet is traveling toward the sun! The tour agent for comets will tell us about these spectacular visitors.

TA: [Comet] (*Tour agent for comets tells the information about them.*)

COM: As we travel back to Earth, we will pass through the asteroid belt again. Follow the instructions of the flight attendant in case of any emergency.

PA 1: That doesn't sound very good. I think the commander is expecting trouble.

PL: A small asteroid is headed this way, Commander.

COM: Activate protection shield and close the shield over the window.

SH: (*Throw the tennis ball through the window and break the bottle at the same time. Drop the white paper shield over the window.*)

FA: Everyone please stay seated and remain calm. The commander and pilot will handle this emergency.

COM: (*After window shield is down.*) That was a little close, but everything is under control. We should be landing on Earth shortly. Sorry about all that excitement.

PL: Landing strip in sight.

COM: Welcome back to Earth, the best planet in the solar system!

Resources

Related Books

Cole, Joanna. *The Magic School Bus® Lost in the Solar System.* Scholastic, Inc., 1990. This delightful book takes children on a unique field trip through the solar system aboard the Magic Bus. They travel past each of the nine planets and the asteroid belt.

Dickinson, Terence. *Exploring the Night Sky.* Firefly Books, 1987. This award-winning children's book contains a step-by-step cosmic voyage from Earth to a distance of 300 million light years, as well as detailed investigations of the planets and information about observing constellations.

Gallant, Roy A. *Our Universe.* National Geographic, 1994. This outstanding picture atlas includes chapters for each of the planets, illustrated with NASA photographs and excellent information about deep space objects, shuttles, and future space exploration.

Kerrod, Robin. *The Illustrated History of NASA.* Gallery Books, 1986. This beautifully illustrated book tells the story of space flight from Dr. Robert Goddard to the future of space exploration. The text is easy to read and filled with little-known information about this period.

Mammana, Dennis. *The Night Sky.* Running Press, 1989. This book provides interesting and easy-to-do investigations and observations of the constellations, planets, moons, and stars.

Sneider, Cary I. *Earth, Moon, and Stars.* Great Explorations in Math and Science (GEMS), Lawrence Hall of Science, 1986, order from NSTA (see Related Materials section). This teacher's guide includes activities related to early concepts of astronomy, Earth's shape and gravity, moon phases and eclipses, and star maps.

Van Cleave, Janice. *Astronomy for Every Kid.* John Wiley & Sons, Inc., 1991. Included are activities and projects with a list of materials, instructions, expected results, and explanations.

Young, Greg. *Exploring Mars and Beyond.* Teacher Created Materials, Inc., 1998. (800) 662-4321. This teacher's guide includes hands-on activities related to the Mars *Pathfinder* and Mars *Global Surveyor* missions for students in grades 5–7.

Young, Ruth M. *Science/Literature Unit: The Magic School Bus,® Lost in the Solar System.* Teacher Created Materials, Inc., 1996. This teacher's guide contains a variety of hands-on activities to teach astronomy concepts, including a script for a simulation flight to a station on the moon.

Young, Ruth M. *Science Simulations: Challenging.* Teacher Created Materials, Inc., 1997. Simulations include a trip to Mars in the year 2025, as well as communicating with intelligent life beyond our solar system.

Related Materials

Astronomical Society of the Pacific, 390 Ashton Ave., San Francisco, CA 94112. http://www.aspsky.org/html/tnl/tnl.html. Publishes the quarterly newsletter *The Universe in the Classroom,* which has a different topic in each issue with background information and lesson ideas. Free to teachers. Supplies materials such as Mars map, booklets, posters, and slides of planets. Request free catalog.

Delta Education, PO Box 3000, Nashua, NH 03071-3000. (800)442-5444. Supplies science materials including solar system mobile, videos such as *America in Space* and *Space Shuttle Pioneers*, astronomy guides, and hands-on kits.

Jet Propulsion Laboratory (JPL), Mail Stop CS-530, 4800 Oak Grove Drive, Pasadena, CA 91109. (818)354-6111. Offers videotapes and pictures on a wide range of topics related to Mars exploration. The video *JPL Computer Graphics* (100 minutes) includes an animation of a flight over Mars, taken from the data gathered during the Viking missions. Excellent photographs with information on the

Resources *(cont.)*

Mars missions. Contact the Teacher Resource Center at JPL, and request that they send material they have on the Mars explorations.

NASA's Central Operation of Resource for Educators (CORE), Lorain County JVS, 15181 Route 28 South, Oberlin, OH 44074, (216)774-1051, Ext. 293. Provides material from NASA to use with students, including slides, videos, and photographs taken from satellites and space missions. Free catalog; send request on school letterhead.

National Geographic Society, PO Box 2118, Washington, DC 20013-2118. (800)447-0647. Supplies maps and posters such as The Heavens, The Earth's Moon, Solar System/Celestial Family, and The Universe. Back issues of *National Geographic* may be ordered. Call for catalog.

National Science Teachers Associations (NSTA). (800) 722-NSTA. Supplies books, posters, and CD-ROMs related to astronomy and other sciences. Order a free catalog of NSTA books and materials.

The Planetary Society, 65 North Catalina Ave., Pasadena, CA 91106-9899. (818) 793-5100. Order the 25 x 45-inch map of Mars, *An Explorer's Guide to Mars.* This map shows details of the planet, as well as pictures from Viking 1 and 2 missions. Request a catalog of other materials.

Sky Calendar, illustrated monthly calendar of daily astronomical events. Annual subscription from Abrams Planetarium, Michigan State University, East Lansing, MI 48824.

Related Web Sites

Astronomy Cafe

http://www2.ari.net/home/odenwald/cafe.html

Sten Odenwald, NASA-Goddard scientist, has listed 3,001 questions he answered about astronomical things. You can ask him new questions as well. There is also an outreach and public information site for NASA's Image spacecraft and includes science activities for educators and images of the space environment of Earth and sun/Earth interactions.

Boeing International Space Station Information

http://www.boeing.com/defense-space/space/spacestation/description.html

Links to specific information and pictures of International Space Station.

Center for Mars Exploration

http://cmex-www.arc.nasa.gov/

NASA's Ames Research Center presents one of the best maintained Mars Web sites. Award-winning home page provides more than 65 links to Mars-related information divided into 15 categories. Check here for latest information about *Pathfinder* and *Global Surveyor.* This includes press releases, backgrounds, and many image links for complete in-depth coverage of Mars-related activities.

Kennedy Space Center Home Page

http://www.ksc.nasa.gov/ksc.html

Information regarding Mercury, Gemini, Apollo, Apollo-Soyuz, and space shuttle program.

Mars Exploration Program

http://www.jpl.nasa.gov/mars/

The Jet Propulsion Laboratory (JPL) offers comprehensive information about Mars exploration projects and related points of interest. Four main areas of exploration provide details on different aspects of the Mars missions. The Mars Exploration Education page is excellent for educators.

Resources *(cont.)*

Mir Space Station Web Site

http://www.hq.nasa.gov/osf/mir/

Links to further information and pictures of Mir.

NASA Educators' Web Site

http://www.hq.nasa/office/codef/education/index.html

National Space Science Data Center

http://nssdc.gsfc.gov/planetary

This is NASA's archive for lunar and planetary data and images. At this site you can find out about past missions to the moon, Mars, and other planets, as well as a chronology of lunar and planetary exploration.

Astronomy Information

http://www.astro.wisc.edu/~dolan/astronomy.html

Location of planets in constellations for the first day of each month for years from 1900–2000

http://www.astro.wisc.edu/~dolan/Planets/planet-const.cgi?year=1997

Links to NASA sites, astronomy, planets, Hubble telescope information, and astronomical education resources

http:\\www.astro.wisc.edu/astro_links.html

Abrams Planetarium Sky Calendar Web site.

http://www.pa.msu.edu/abrams/diary.html

Gives a sample Sky Calendar and Night Sky and has current things to watch for during the month, moon phases with specific date/time

Moons Phases Through Time

http://www.naturalist.net/Moon_Phases_through_time.htm

Views of the Solar System and History of Space Exploration

http://www.hawastsoc.org/solar/eng/homepage.htm

CD-ROMs

Eyewitness Encyclopedia of Space and the Universe. DK Multimedia, New York, NY. (800)356-6575. http://www.dk.com. (Also available from ASP, listed under Related Materials.) Visually exciting learning adventure into outer space aboard *Skylab* for a day, also a 3-D model of the space station *Mir.* Learn how it feels to live in space. Ages 7+.

Views of the Solar System, National Science Teachers Association, Arlington, VA. (800)722-NATA. A fantastic resource for everyone from young students to adults. It is like an Internet Web page with hypertext links and comes with *Microsoft Internet Explorer.* It contains information about sun, moon, planets, asteroids, comets, and meteors and detailed views of the solar system. Click on Jupiter, for example, and you get information about each of the giant planet's 16 moons and the impact of fragments of comet *Shoemaker-Levy 9.* It even includes a recipe for making a model comet nucleus with dry ice and a few other simple ingredients.

Answer Key

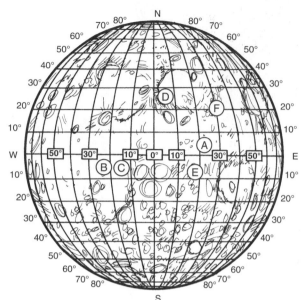

Pages 51 and 52 (Planets of the Gods)

The symbols for each of the planets are shown below. The information regarding the gods for which they are named will vary. Sources for this information are the book *Our Universe* (See the Resources section.) and encyclopedias.

Planet Symbols and Gods			
Mercury ☿	wings Messenger of the Roman gods	**Jupiter** ♃	lightning bolt King of Roman gods
Venus ♀	hand mirror Roman goddess of love and beauty	**Saturn** ♄	curved sickle Roman god of reaping, father of Jupiter
Earth ⊕	Greek for sphere Greek goddess Earth Mother	**Uranus** ⛢	sign for the metal platinum Roman father of Saturn
Mars ♂	shield and spear Roman god of war	**Neptune** ♆	trident: fishing spear Roman god of the ocean
Pluto ♇	PL: Pluto and Percival Lowell (Pluto was discovered at Lowell Observatory in 1930.) Greek god of the dark underworld		

Page 62

Circumference (measured to nearest cm)	Diameter	= Results
15.5 cm	5 cm	3.10
25.3 cm	8 cm	3.16
38 cm	12 cm	3.17
Answers will vary.		

Diameter of the Earth 7,973 miles x 3.14 = 25,035 miles (circumference) ÷ 24 hours = 1,043 mph.

Page 63

	Circumference	÷ Hours in a Day	= Miles Per Hour
Mercury	9,577	1,416	6.76
Venus	23,747.82	5,832	4.07
Earth	25,035.22	24	1,043.13
Mars	13,332.44	25	533.30
Jupiter	280,606.1	10	28,060.61
Saturn	236,551.9	11	21,504.72
Uranus	100,285.32	17	5,899.14
Neptune	97,145.32	16	6,071.58
Pluto	4,515.32	153	29.51